# The **Essential** Buyer's Guide

## AUDI
# TT

### All Mk1 (8N) models 1998-2006

Your marque expert:
Mark Davies

T0386772

## VELOCE PUBLISHING
THE PUBLISHER OF FINE AUTOMOTIVE BOOKS

Essential Buyer's Guide Series
Alfa GT (Booker)
Alfa Romeo Spider Giulia (Booker & Talbott)
Audi TT (Davies)
Austin Seven (Barker)
Big Healeys (Trummel)
BMW E21 3 Series (1975-1983) (Reverente, Cook)
BMW GS (Henshaw)
BMW X5 (Saunders)
BSA 500 & 650 Twins (Henshaw)
BSA Bantam (Henshaw)
Citroën 2CV (Paxton)
Citroën ID & DS (Heilig)
Cobra Replicas (Ayre)
Corvette C2 Sting Ray 1963-1967 (Falconer)
Ducati Bevel Twins (Falloon)
Ducati Desmodue Twins (Falloon)
Ducati Desmoquattro Twins (Falloon)
Fiat 500 & 600 (Bobbitt)
Ford Capri (Paxton)
Ford Escort Mk1 & Mk2 (Williamson)
Ford Mustang (Cook)
Ford RS Cosworth Sierra & Escort (Williamson)
Harley-Davidson Big Twins (Henshaw)
Hinckley Triumph triples & fours 750, 900, 955, 1000,
1050, 1200 – 1991-2009 (Henshaw)
Honda CBR600 Hurricane (Henshaw)
Honda CBR FireBlade (Henshaw)
Honda SOHC fours 1969-1984 (Henshaw)
Jaguar E-type 3.8 & 4.2-litre (Crespin)
Jaguar E-type V12 5.3-litre (Crespin)
Jaguar XJ 1995-2003 (Crespin)
Jaguar XK8 & XKR (1996-2005) (Thorley)
Jaguar/Daimler XJ6, XJ12 & Sovereign (Crespin)
Jaguar/Daimler XJ40 (Crespin)
Jaguar Mark 1 & 2 (All models including Daimler 2.5-litre
V8) 1955 to 1969 (Thorley)
Jaguar S-type – 1999 to 2007 (Thorley)
Jaguar X-type – 2001 to 2009 (Thorley)
Jaguar XJ-S (Crespin)
Jaugar XJ6, XJ8 & XJR (Thorley)
Jaguar XK 120, 140 & 150 (Thorley)

Kawasaki Z1 & Z900 (Orritt)
Land Rover Series I, II & IIA (Thurman)
Land Rover Series III (Thurman)
Lotus Seven replicas & Caterham 7: 1973-2013 (Hawkins)
Mazda MX-5 Miata (Mk1 1989-97 & Mk2 98-2001) (Crook)
Mercedes-Benz 280SL-560DSL Roadsters (Bass)
Mercedes-Benz 'Pagoda' 230SL, 250SL & 280SL
MGA 1955-1962 (Sear, Crosier)
MGF & MG TF (Hawkins)
MGB & MGB GT (Williams)
MG Midget & A-H Sprite (Horler)
MG TD, TF & TF1500 (Jones)
Mini (Paxton)
Morris Minor & 1000 (Newell)
New Mini (Collins)
Norton Commando (Henshaw)
Peugeot 205 GTI (Blackburn)
Porsche 911 (930) Turbo series (Streather)
Porsche 911 (964) (Streather)
Porsche 911 (993) (Streather)
Porsche 911 (996) (Streather)
Porsche 911 Carrera 3.2 series 1984 to 1989 (Streather)
Porsche 911SC – Coupé, Targa, Cabriolet & RS Model
years 1978-1983 (Streather)
Porsche 924 – All models 1976 to 1988 (Hodgkins)
Porsche 928 (Hemmings)
Porsche 930 Turbo & 911 (930) Turbo (Streather)
Porsche 944 (Higgins, Mitchell)
Porsche 986 Boxster series (Streather)
Porsche 987 Boxster and Cayman series (Streather)
Rolls-Royce Silver Shadow & Bentley T-Series (Bobbitt)
Subaru Impreza (Hobbs)
Triumph Bonneville (Henshaw)
Triumph Stag (Mort & Fox)
Triumph TR7 & TR8 (Williams)
Triumph Thunderbird, Trophy & Tiger (Henshaw)
Vespa Scooters – Classic two-stroke models 1960-2008
(Paxton)
Volvo 700/900 Series (Beavis)
VW Beetle (Cservenka & Copping)
VW Bus (Cservenka & Copping)
VW Golf GTI (Cservenka & Copping)

# www.veloce.co.uk

For post publication news, updates and amendments relating to this book please visit www.veloce.co.uk/book/V4614

First published in March 2014 by Veloce Publishing Limited, Veloce House, Parkway Farm Business Park, Middle Farm Way, Poundbury, Dorchester, Dorset, DT1 3AR, England.
Fax 01305 250479/e-mail info@veloce.co.uk/web www.veloce.co.uk or www.velocebooks.com.
ISBN: 978-1-845846-14-5 UPC: 6-36847-04614-9

Readers with ideas for automotive books, or books on other transport or related hobby subjects, are invited to write to the editorial director of Veloce Publishing at the above address.
British Library Cataloguing in Publication Data – A catalogue record for this book is available from the British Library.
Typesetting, design and page make-up all by Veloce Publishing Ltd on Apple Mac. Printed in India by Imprint Digital Ltd.

# Introduction
## – the purpose of this book

In the modern motor industry, with brand design cues and corporate signatures, it's unusual for a car design to be truly ground-breaking, but one rare example is certainly the Audi TT. When the original concept was first unveiled at the Frankfurt Motor Show in 1995, it was clear that here was a classic straight from the drawing board. Its influence on the design of cars that followed makes it difficult to appreciate, nearly two decades later, just how radical its concept was at the time. Few concepts make it to production in their original incarnations, but when the first production car was launched in 1998, aside from the introduction of a quarter-light behind the door windows of the coupé and some minor changes to the front bumper, very little had changed. The original design ethos had survived intact, and the profile lines of the car, which have since become truly iconic, remained as originally intended.

It was the beauty of the car, both its exterior and interior, that assured its success, and it immediately sold in large numbers. The TT became the must-have sports coupé of the new millennium, with buyers prepared to pay considerable premiums to get their hands on one. Years later, the TT can still turn heads and attract admiring glances or appreciative comments on fuel station forecourts. The term 'design icon' may well be overused, but in the case of the Audi TT it is certainly well deserved. Consequently, the TT invariably features high on any list of future car classics.

The original concept car, as shown at Frankfurt in 1995. (Courtesy Audi UK)

The TT is no slouch either. Based on the platform of the VW Golf GTI, it came with a decades-long pedigree for spirited and sporty road driving. It's not a supercar, but with up to 240bhp available from the turbocharged engine, it has more than enough performance to put a smile on your face. Fitted with Audi's celebrated AWD quattro system, developed for motorsport and overwhelmingly successful in that field, the handling is impressive. The car is not without flaws, but putting a beautiful body and interior onto such a successful chassis was always likely to be a winning formula, and there is no doubt that the TT instantly won the hearts of the car-buying public.

The overwhelming success of the car does however create issues when buying secondhand. Some people bought the TT as a fashion accessory, so many cars have had owners who wouldn't consider themselves to be motoring enthusiasts. Therefore, not all TTs have been looked after as well as they might have been, and care needs to be taken to avoid buying an example that will soon start costing large sums of money to keep on the road. This guide is intended to help you in the buying process, to avoid buying those poor examples that are certainly out there, and hopefully find that gem that will provide you enjoyment for many years as the TT matures as an all-time classic.

The TT was an instant success and became the must-have coupé of the new millennium. (Courtesy Karen Isherwood-Clemens)

## Acknowledgements

With thanks to the members of the TTOC who provided images, and in particular to Scott, Karen and Mark, who made their cars available for the workshop photos. Also thanks to Bob Lafebre for research in the USA, and to John at Awesome GTI in the UK and Alex Fisk at Audi UK, who were very helpful with vital information.

Particular thanks to Shak Shivji and Lowndes Street Garage for invaluable technical advice and use of their workshop facilities.

Screenshot images from VCDS (VAG-COM Diagnostic System) reproduced by kind permission of Ross-Tech.

Unless stated all other images by Mark and Debbie Davies.

# Contents

**Introduction**
– the purpose of this book .. .. .. .. .. 3

**1 Is it the right car for you?**
– marriage guidance .. .. .. .. .. .. 6

**2 Cost considerations**
– affordable, or a money pit? .. .. .. .. 7

**3 Living with a TT**
– will you get along together? . .. .. .. 8

**4 Relative values**
– which model for you? .. .. .. .. .. .10

**5 Before you view**
– be well informed .. .. .. .. .. .. .13

**6 Inspection equipment**
– these items will really help .. .. .. .16

**7 Fifteen minute evaluation**
– walk away or stay? .. .. .. .. .. .17

**8 Key points**
– where to look for problems .. .. .. .23

**9 Serious evaluation**
– 60 minutes for years of enjoyment .24

**10 Auctions**
– sold! Another way to buy your
dream. .. .. .. .. .. .. .. .. .. .42

**11 Paperwork**
– correct documentation is
essential! .. .. .. .. .. .. .. .. .44

**12 What's it worth?**
– let your head rule your heart .. .. .47

**13 Do you really want to
restore?**
– it'll take longer and cost more
than you think. .. .. .. .. .. .. .. .49

**14 Paint problems**
– bad complexion, including dimples,
pimples and bubbles .. .. .. .. .. .51

**15 Problems due to lack of use**
– just like their owners, TTs need
exercise! . .. .. .. .. .. .. .. .. .53

**16 The Community**
– key people, organisations and
companies in the Audi world .. .. .. .55

**17 Vital statistics**
– essential data at your fingertips .. .57

**Index** .. .. .. .. .. .. .. .. .. .64

**The Essential Buyer's Guide™ currency**
At the time of publication a BG unit of currency "  " equals approximately
£1.00/US $1.63/Euro 1.20 Please adjust to suit current exchange rates
using Sterling as the base currency.

## 1 Is it the right car for you?
– marriage guidance

The TT is 4041mm long and 1764mm wide (159.1in x 69.4in), so will fit in most single-car garages. As with most coupés, the doors are longer than most, so will need room to open.

The ride is firm, though not harsh. The power steering is light enough for any driver, while still giving a feel for the road. The manual gearbox is precise with a light clutch, and the DSG automatic provides seamless and effortless gear changes. The assisted brakes need little effort.

A car both beautiful and practical, and easy to live with every day. (Courtesy Josh Dennison)

The standard seats are supportive and comfortable, and in most examples come heated. There is plenty of adjustment, and the car easily accommodates drivers over 6ft. The Recaro seats fitted to the QS are firmer, narrower, and have less adjustment. There is ample rake and reach movement for the steering wheel, so most people can find a comfortable driving position.

The rear seats of the 2+2 coupé are suitable only for young children or small adults. An Isofix system is available for child seats.

The boot of both the coupé and the roadster is large enough for two suitcases, and the rear seats of the coupé fold down flat, providing room for a surprisingly large amount of luggage.

Performance-wise, 0-62mph comes in 6.6s with a top speed of 151mph.

The TT has a generous boot. Here is the author's car loaded up for a scuba diving trip.

If driven conservatively, fuel economy of 30mpg can be achieved, though $CO_2$ emissions are high at 226g/km. Insurance premiums are above average, though specialist insurers will offer limited mileage policies.

Parts are readily available, and there is a healthy network of independent VAG (Volkswagen Audi Group) specialists to look after your car.

# 2 Cost considerations
– affordable, or a money pit?

The TT has a variable service schedule – the car runs self-diagnostics and lets you know when it needs a service, but the maximum interval is 19,000 miles.

|  | 1.8T | V6 |
| --- | --- | --- |
| Interim service | x150 | x190 |
| Full service | x240 | x300 |
| Haldex service | x125 | x125 |
| Brake discs and pads | x300 | x925 |
| Wheel alignment | x150 | x150 |
|  |  |  |
| Replace suspension |  |  |
| OEM | x1135 | x1135 |
| Performance | x600 | x600 |
| Coilovers | x680 | x680 |
|  |  |  |
| Exhaust | x795 | x795 |
| Clutch/flywheel | x1195 | x1195 |
| Remap | x635 |  |
| Turbo refurbishment | x1740 |  |
| Suspension bushes | x785 | x785 |
| DSG service |  | x225 |

A V6 engine block removed from the car and ready for work. (Courtesy Steve Collier)

Prices quoted are for parts and labour, presuming genuine parts unless otherwise stated. All parts are still readily available.

A DSG gearbox stripped down. This one is being uprated to deal with increased engine power. (Courtesy Steve Collier)

The well-presented engine from a multiple show-winning car.

# 3 Living with a TT
– will you get along together?

The TT is a really beautiful car, inside and out. Just sitting in it and seeing the well-designed dash, with machined aluminium dials on the air vents, and letting your palm rest on the aluminium gear knob is enough to bring a smile to your face. Even after years of ownership it seems impossible to park the car and walk away from it without turning round to give it a brief, admiring glance. In short, it's a car that is a joy to just be in and to own, and that is very much at the heart of its appeal.

In terms of driving experience, it does have its critics. Some suggest it is less engaging than a true sports car should be, and, in truth, there is some merit in that argument. Audi has a reputation for building cars that feel safe,

A 225 Roadster out in the country on a sunny day. Does it get any better than this? (Courtesy Ian Manson)

based mostly on its AWD quattro system. It is essentially a front-wheel drive system, with the rear wheels engaging once a loss of grip is detected. This does make the car feel firmly planted, but with a tendency for understeer, so arguably less exciting than a more traditional front-engined, rear wheel-driven configuration. However, the grip provided by the quattro system is impressive, and provides its own enjoyment in the corners. With Audi's Electronic Stability Program (ESP) engaged, you can confidently probe the limits of both the car and your ability to get the most out of your drive. It's not a car that you can readily drive sideways, but it does reward you in other ways.

It is perfectly adequate as a daily driver, and indeed with the driver's seat being such an enjoyable place to be, even the most congested traffic conditions become endurable. For the purpose of commuting, it is certainly not the most economical of cars by current standards, but if this is an important factor to you, the 180 offers a more frugal option when compared with the relatively thirsty 3.2 V6.

Longer journeys are covered with ease – especially with cruise control, which may have been factory fitted as an option, or can be retrofitted with OEM parts relatively cheaply.

The TT isn't littered with these sort of toys, however. Seat adjustment is manual, parking sensors are not

The beautifully designed interior can be very enticing to a prospective buyer.

included, nor does it have automatic headlights or windscreen wipers – all of which could be found on less prestigious contemporary vehicles. Satellite navigation was an option which was rarely taken up, as Audi's system was not considered particularly good compared with the aftermarket options available at the time. In addition to the heated seats there are heated wing mirrors, and there is an effective air-conditioning system, though again, that is not a dual climate system that you may have found on other cars of its time. A BOSE sound system can be found in most examples, but not all. The TT is not a luxury car, but then nor is it weighed down with performance-hampering gadgets: it's all you need it to be, with little that you don't need.

The TT benefits from Audi's long-life service programme. In essence, the car monitors itself and lets you know when it needs a service. Intervals can reach a maximum of 19,000 miles, though it is essential to use the right oil. The system can be reset to be serviced every 10,000 miles or 12 months, which may be advisable as the car gets older. Servicing costs from the Audi dealer network can be expensive, but there are many independent VAG specialists who can provide an excellent service at greatly reduced cost.

If maintained properly, the TT is a well-built, robust, and reliable car. It is a complex piece of motor engineering though, with a great deal of electronics managing the engine, the quattro drive system, and other driver aids and safety features. In time, the sensors for those systems can fail, but diagnosing faults is greatly aided by interrogating the car's computer systems. That means the car needs more than basic mechanical knowledge to maintain it, but that does not mean it is beyond the abilities of an enthusiastic amateur with a reasonable degree of knowledge, equipped with the necessary diagnostic software. There are excellent internet forums from which expert advice on all problems can be gleaned, and again, because the TT shares its basic platform with the very popular MK4 VW Golf GTI, there are many VAG specialist tuners who will know the TT inside out.

I have been using a TT as a daily driver for a decade, covering up to 15,000 miles a year, and it has very rarely suffered any problems. If you are looking for a relatively modern and reliable classic that can be used on a regular or even daily basis, this may well be the car for you.

It's hard to walk away from the TT without looking back for an admiring glance.
(Courtesy Jorge Enrique)

# 4 Relative values
– which model for you?

225, Quattro Sport or V6 – the engine is usually the first consideration when deciding which car to buy.

The TT is part of the post-hot hatch sports car revival. Its buyers demanded the same comforts and practicality that they got with the hot hatches, which, in the 1980s, all but caused the complete demise of the traditional two seat convertible sports car. As a result, contrary to usual convention, the coupé was just as popular as the roadster, and

The 225 coupé is the most common example. Some colours are rarer than others, and are often sought-after. (Courtesy Karen Isherwood-Clemens)

today's values still reflect that. In the case of the TT, it is not the roof (or absence of one) that has the most significant influence on its value, but rather the engine that drives it.

Post-2002 models with a better standard specification are preferred. The limited numbers and performance of the QS commands a premium. Likewise, the 3.2 V6 is popular not only for the extra power and sound, but also for the DSG gearbox only ever fitted with that engine – though 3.2 manuals, being rare, are also sought-after.

The 225s are by far the most common, and plentiful supply keeps values down. The 180s are less common (except as roadsters), and some prefer the free revving engine with its lighter turbo, and may pay a higher price for it.

The entry-level 150 has limited appeal, and is therefore the cheapest to buy.

For fans of open-top motoring, there is the roadster. Most commonly found with the 180 engine, but all options are available.
(Courtesy Phillip Evans)

The model had a face-lift in 2002. Earlier cars had the five-bar front grille and traditional windscreen wipers.

Lightweight, limited numbers, and the most powerful engine make the Quattro Sport the most desirable for some, but limited practicality rule it out for others.
(Courtesy Scott Isherwood)

The S-Line had a limited production run, until the extras it offered became standard equipment in 2002. They can be identified by the badge forward of the rear wheelarch.

| Year | 1998 | 1999 | 2000 | 2001 | **2002** | 2003 | 2004 | 2005 | 2006 |
|---|---|---|---|---|---|---|---|---|---|
| Weighting | -10 | -10 | -5 | -5 | **0** | 0 | +5 | +10 | +10 |
| **Body** | | | | | | | | | |
| Coupé | 0 | 0 | 0 | 0 | **0** | 0 | 0 | 0 | 0 |
| Roadster | 0 | 0 | 0 | 0 | **0** | 0 | 0 | 0 | 0 |
| **Engine** | | | | | | | | | |
| 150 | | | | | **-10** | -10 | -10 | -10 | -10 |
| 180 | -5 | -5 | -5 | -5 | **-5** | -5 | -5 | -5 | -5 |
| 225 | 0 | 0 | 0 | 0 | **0** | 0 | 0 | 0 | 0 |
| V6 | | | | | | +5 | +5 | +5 | +5 |
| QS | | | | | | | | +5 | +5 |

Taking the post face-lift 2002 225 coupé as the benchmark model, the adjustments shown provide relative values of other models by comparison. For example (working vertically downward from the year), a 2005 V6 Coupé would be worth +10+0+5 = 15% more, but a 2000 180 Roadster -5+0-5 = 10% less than a 2002 225 Coupé. These are general comparatives and assume all the cars are in the same condition.

Heavily modified cars are a personal choice. They are often difficult to sell, but maybe there's one out there which is exactly what you're looking for.

A beautiful and rare ABT-bodied 225 coupé. There are very few genuine examples of these available.

# 5 Before you view

– be well informed

Going to view the car you end up buying can be a great experience, so be clear about the answers you want to hear before you hand over your cash. In addition to the considerations below, making a list of the questions most important to you and getting them answered by a short email or call to the seller, can often save you the disappointment of a wasted journey.

Don't forget to check the current values of the models you are interested in, using car magazines that feature price guides. Online sale listings and auction sites can also be a great way to get a feel for how general condition and model specific extras can affect prices.

### Where is the car?

Is it going to be worth travelling some distance to view the car? Having received an email response or talked with the seller by phone, you'll be better able to judge their appreciation of the journey you'll have to make, and how accommodating they're likely to be for your assessments when you arrive.

Models closer to home may not be exactly what you're looking for, but the little effort involved will provide you with invaluable experience for the more important candidate to come. You may even be surprised by what you find locally.

### Dealer or private sale?

Establish early on if a car is being sold by its owner or by a trader. A private owner should have all the history. A dealer may have more limited knowledge of a car's history, but should have some documentation. A dealer may offer a warranty/ guarantee (ask for a printed copy), and finance.

### Cost of collection and delivery?

A dealer may well be used to quoting for delivery by car transporter. A private owner may agree to meet you halfway, but only agree to this after you have seen the car at the vendor's address to validate the documents. You could meet halfway and agree the sale, but insist on meeting at the vendor's address for the handover.

### View: when and where?

It is always preferable to view at the vendor's home or business premises. In the case of a private sale, the car's documentation should tally with the vendor's name and address. Arrange to view only in daylight and avoid a wet day: most cars look better in poor light or when wet.

### Reason for sale?

Do make it one of the first questions you ask. Why is the car being sold, and how long has it been with the current owner? How many previous owners have there been?

### Conversions & modifications?

Modified examples, or those with replacement or different engines fitted must be given further attention to determine the reason for the changes, the suitability and compatibility of non-original parts, and the competency of those that undertook the work.

## Condition?

Ask for an honest appraisal of the car's condition. Ask specifically about some of the check items described in chapter 7.

## All original specification?

An original equipment car is normally of higher value than a customized version. However some modifications can add value due to the benefits and rarity of the parts involved. For example, if an M90 gearbox has been fitted to a 740 to modernize the gear shifting and do away with the overdrive, this can add value due to the quality and rarity of the gearbox. As always, be sure of the age and condition of any parts changed as well as seeking conformation of a proficient fitment, such as a receipt from a reputable mechanic.

## Matching data/legal ownership?

Do the VIN/chassis, engine numbers and licence plate match the official registration documents? For those countries that require an annual test of roadworthiness, does the car have a document showing that it complies? (an MOT certificate in the UK, which can be verified on 0845 600 5977)

If a smog/emissions certificate is mandatory, does the car have one? If required, does the car carry a current road fund licence plate tag?

Does the vendor own the car outright? Money might be owed to a finance company or bank; the car could even be stolen. For a fee, several organizations will supply the ownership data, based on the car's licence plate number. Such companies can often also tell you if a car has been 'written-off' by an insurance company. The following organizations can supply data:

HPI ... .. .. .. .. .. .. .. .. .. .. .. .. .. .. .. .. .. .. .. . 01722 422 422 (UK)
AA . .. .. .. .. .. .. .. .. .. .. .. .. .. .. .. .. .. .. .. .. . 0870 600 0836 (UK)
DVLA . .. .. .. .. .. .. .. .. .. .. .. .. .. .. .. .. .. .. .. . 0870 240 0010 (UK)
RAC .. .. .. .. .. .. .. .. .. .. .. .. .. .. .. .. .. .. .. .. . 0870 533 3660 (UK)
Carfax .. .. .. .. .. .. .. .. .. .. .. .. .. .. .. .. .. http://www.carfax.com (USA)
Autocheck . .. .. .. .. .. .. .. .. .. .. .. .. .. .. http://www.autocheck.com (USA)

Other countries will have similar organizations.

## Insurance?

Check with your existing insurer before setting out, as your current policy might not cover you to drive the car if you do purchase it.

## How you can pay

A cheque will take several days to clear and the seller may prefer to sell to a cash buyer. However, a bankers draft (a cheque issued by a bank) is as good as cash but safer, so contact your own bank and become familiar with formalities that are necessary to obtain one.

## Buying at auction

If the intention is to buy at auction, see chapter 10 for further advice.

## Professional vehicle check (mechanical examination)

There are often marque/model specialists who will undertake professional examination of a vehicle on your behalf. Owners' clubs will be able to put you in touch with such specialists. Other organizations that will carry out a general professional check include:

AA. .. .. .. .. .. 0800 085 3007 (UK motoring organization with vehicle inspectors)
ABS .. .. .. .. .. .. .. 0800 358 5855 (UK specialist vehicle inspection company)
RAC .. .. .. .. .. 0870 533 3660 (UK motoring organization with vehicle inspectors)
AAA .http://www.aaa.com (USA motoring organization with vehicle inspection centres)

Other countries will have similar organizations.

A tastefully modified coupé photographed at night. (Courtesy David Tonks)

# 6 Inspection equipment
– these items will really help

Before you rush out of the door, gather together a few items that will help as you work your way around the car.

**This book**
**Reading glasses (if you need them for close work)**
**Magnet (not powerful, a fridge magnet is ideal)**
**Torch (flashlight)**
**Probe (a small screwdriver works very well)**
**Overalls**
**Mirror on a stick**
**Digital camera/camera phone**
**Fault code scanner**
**A friend, preferably a knowledgeable enthusiast**

A scanner can be used to detect faults recorded on the car's ECU.

This book is designed to be your guide at every step, so take it along and use the check boxes to help you assess each area of the car you're interested in. Don't be afraid to let the seller see you using it.

You may need reading glasses to read documents and make close up inspections.

A torch with fresh batteries will be useful for peering into the wheelarches and under the car.

A small screwdriver can be used – with care – as a probe, particularly along any dirt covered chassis rails. With this you should be able to check any areas of severe corrosion, but be careful – if it's really bad the screwdriver might go right through the metal!

Be prepared to get dirty. Take along a pair of overalls, if you have them, and a few pairs of disposable gloves.

Fixing a mirror at an angle on the end of a stick may seem odd, but you'll probably need it to check the condition of the underside of the car. It will also help you to peer into some of the important crevices. You can use it, together with the torch, along the underside of the chassis and floor. You're looking for accident damage, signs of where the car has bottomed out, and corrosion.

If you have a digital camera, take it along so that you can later study some areas of the car closely. You can even hold it under the car to take pictures of areas you cannot see. Take a picture of any part of the car that causes you concern, and seek a friend or specialist's opinion.

Ideally, have a friend or knowledgeable enthusiast accompany you: a second opinion is always valuable. If nobody is available, find out if you can call someone when inspecting the car who can offer advice.

Use either a laptop computer with suitable software installed and connected with an OBD2 cable or a purpose-built scanner designed for VAG cars to detect fault codes.

# 7 Fifteen minute evaluation
– walk away or stay?

With its stunning good looks, a TT purchase is often made by the heart. When considering a car, it's very important not to let yourself get carried away. Try to be thoroughly objective about your decision – even just getting into one of these seductive cars (the interior is especially appealing) can be highly persuasive when it comes to the buying decision. Be very wary of buying the first car you see, and try and look at as many as you can. Comparing different examples gives you a much better idea of which are worth a closer look, and which are best avoided – if the first one turns out to be the best you can always go back. Try out the various engine derivatives – all have merits, and you may be surprised which suits you best. Fortunately there isn't a shortage of supply, so there are normally plenty of TTs to choose from on the market, providing you are prepared to travel a little.

Seeing the correct paperwork for the car should be your first concern. There should be an owner's registration document, and in most countries, a certificate of roadworthiness obtained from a periodic inspection, usually annually. These inspections, such as the MoT in the United Kingdom, do have a limited scope, so even a recent inspection cannot be relied upon exclusively as evidence that the car is in perfect working order. A roadworthiness certificate is a legal requirement, and you would be taking a risk buying a car without one. If the car does not have a test certificate there may be a very expensive reason why, and the car is best avoided. In some countries, including the UK, the certificate will record problems which, though not matters resulting in a test failure, are still areas of concern. These are often referred to as 'advisories.' Have a discussion with the seller to find out whether the matters raised have been addressed, and, where available, check invoices for any work done.

Unlike the more 'traditional' classic car, the relatively modern TT does not tend to suffer from rust – with many of the body panels made from galvanised steel or aluminium, it is rarely a concern at all. Indeed, as a modern car with an array of sophisticated driver aids, the biggest concern is the car's electronic systems. A multitude of sensors distributed around the car constantly monitor various parameters, which means the car itself can tell you about any serious issues. These can be read by plugging some diagnostic software into the car's ECU via the OBD2 port (which is found above the bonnet release handle located in the driver's footwell). In light of this, it is recommended you take along a laptop computer with the appropriate software and an OBD2 cable to connect it to the car, or a purpose-made fault scanner, even for a quick evaluation.

There are various diagnostic software packages available which can be sourced and downloaded via the internet, and some packages with

A laptop equipped with appropriate software and connected to the OBD port will detect any recorded faults on the car's ECU.

limited, but still very useful capabilities, are available as free shareware. As an alternative, self-contained fault code scanners can be bought quite cheaply, though you need to ensure you get one compatible with Volkswagen Audi Group (VAG) cars. While some specialist knowledge is needed to take that information and remedy the faults, the scan can at least give an indication that a problem exists, making it a very useful tool for the purpose of evaluating

The software available can perform extensive checks of all the systems on the car.

a prospective purchase. Bear in mind however, that both the diagnostic software and the fault scanners can also be used to clear recorded faults from the ECU. Your seller may have access to these, and could have cleared any faults prior to your inspection. It is therefore important to take the car for a test drive prior to scanning it so that any persistent faults get re-recorded onto the ECU. But before you test drive, carry out some basic tests to ensure the car is safe. These checks are invaluable – while a computer scan is perhaps the most revealing test, it can't tell you everything.

Take a walk around the car. Panel fit on a TT is usually excellent, and gaps between panels should be narrow and even. Any variations could indicate poorly completed accident repairs. There is a crease in the doors that runs rearwards from the lower edge of the bonnet to meet the top of the rear wheelarch. Sight along that line, also checking the black plastic strip that runs along the lower edge of the side windows. These lines should be continuous and even: if not, a poorly fitted door could indicate problems. Look for minor dents in the doors and side panels. These can often be picked up from the doors of careless motorists in car parks, and the aluminium panels can be more susceptible to dents than steel. Fortunately, most can be fixed easily and cheaply by specialist dent repairers without resorting to expensive paintwork, however dents in awkward places such as near the edges of doors or through the creases in the body panels can be hard to rectify.

Check for chips in the windscreen. Though this is not a particularly expensive repair, and replacements remain readily available. Also look for damage to the other windows and cracks in the light clusters. Look for signs of condensation in the headlights, indicating a problem with the seals of the units. This problem is not uncommon, and while it can be fixed by taking the headlight apart and re-sealing it, the process is quite a tricky one.

Check the wheels for damage and signs of kerbing. Any wheel damage suggests an impact which could have created problems elsewhere, especially on the front wheels. With the wheels pointing forwards the steering wheel should be positioned dead-centre – if

Check the line of the panel crease running between the wheelarches, and ensure it is straight.

it is not there are wheel alignment issues and potential damage to the steering or suspension elements. An off-centre steering wheel will be even more apparent when driving the car later.

Under the bonnet there are some simple checks to make. First, check the VIN (Vehicle Identification Number). This is stamped centrally into the bulkhead to the rear of the engine bay, beneath a clear window in the plastic scuttle at the lower edge of the windscreen. It is also displayed on a silver sticker to the left of the engine bay. This should show no sign of ever being removed. Curled edges or creases should cause immediate concern. The 17-digit identification number should correspond with both that displayed visibly on the dashboard (seen through the windscreen on the right-hand side), and on the car's registration document. More detailed information can be found in chapter 8 – Key points. If there are any discrepancies at all with these numbers, walk away.

This may sound basic, but make sure the car has the engine you were expecting. A 225 may be more readily distinguished from the less powerful versions by its twin exhaust outlets (as opposed to the single pipe of the 150 and 180), but it is not uncommon for 180s to have been fitted with the twin pipes and rear valance of a 225. The seller may be trying to pass off the car as the more powerful version or, indeed, if they bought the car in that condition, may well not appreciate the difference. The engines are most easily distinguished visibly from the inlet manifolds positioned to the front. On the 225 the throttle body is positioned to the right of the manifold, and on the 150 and 180 it is on the left. Likewise, many 225s have been modified to have the appearance of the limited edition QS, but the genuine examples can be identified from the lack of the battery in the main engine bay. In the QS it has been relocated to the rear of the car to improve weight distribution.

Check the levels of oil, coolant and brake fluids. If they are incorrect, it may indicate a poorly maintained car. The oil should be clear rather than black. Open the oil filler cap and look for deposits of a white, mayonnaise-like substance which could show a blown head gasket. Be aware that in low mileage cars which have only done short journeys this can still appear in the absence of any issues.

Examine the wheels for signs of kerbing or more serious impact damage.

The 180 engine is recognised by the throttle body, positioned to the left side of the inlet manifold to the front of the engine. (Courtesy Jorge Enrique)

Black, tar-like deposits on the underside of the oil filler cap can indicate long intervals between oil changes.

Ask the seller or a friend to start the engine for you, first paying attention to the exhaust tailpipes. On initial start-up look out for signs of bluish smoke being emitted which can indicate problems with the turbo. Listen to the engine. A slight ticking noise when started from cold isn't a problem, though this should disappear after a few seconds.

Getting into the car, first check the upholstery for signs of scuffing. The leather used is of excellent quality and tends to wear very well, so scuff marks on the seats of a car claiming to have relatively low mileage should be a concern. The brushed aluminium contact points of the interior also pick up signs of wear with use, so check the gear knob (if the car has the aluminium version), door releases, and the circular caps at the base of the door pull handles for excessive scratching. Check the adjustment of the seats and steering wheel and ensure you can achieve a comfortable driving position for yourself.

On a genuine QS you should expect to find the battery compartment empty. The battery is located in the boot.

Test the brake pedal. It should feel firm and not travel all the way to the floor. Turn on the ignition and check the DIS (Driver Information System) positioned in the centre of the dash clocks. The LED display can develop faults, apparent by blank lines running though the information displayed. This is repairable, but is a tricky job and can be costly. Presuming the display itself is working fine, check what it tells you. On switching on the ignition, the car does a brief diagnostic self-check. On the right-hand dial all the warning lights show: engine management, ABS, parking brake, and battery. A large yellow 'OK' should appear on the DIS in the centre of the console. If there are issues, any of a number of warning symbols could appear here, in which case check the owner's manual – it could be something as trivial as an empty screen washer bottle, or a more serious matter, such as worn brake pads.

On starting the engine the car performs self-diagnostics and a reassuring 'OK' should appear on the dash.

Assuming everything is fine, the start-up sequence will continue. The ABS lights and the yellow 'OK' should now go out. Start the engine and the engine management and battery lights should now also drop out, leaving you with only the parking brake warning showing.

Check the switches. First try the heated seats to give them a chance to warm up. The dials are in the centre of the dash, together with the hazard warning lights, rear window heater and ESP control. A press on the seat control causes the dial to pop out. Turn it clockwise, and a series of red lights appear around the dial. Leave it on – it takes a few minutes for the seats to warm up. Check the rest of the switchgear, windows, mirrors etc, and ensure they are all working as they should. By now you should be feeling the heat from the seats so presuming they are working, cool off by checking the air-conditioning is functioning properly. The controls are in the centre of the console below the stereo. The left-hand dial controls the temperature. Hold it to the left until the display shows 'LOW,' and ensure cold air is blown from the vents.

If your initial inspection gives you confidence that the car is generally roadworthy, take it for a short drive to get the engine up to working temperature. Within a few minutes of starting from cold the temperature gauge should rise to 90c and stay there. If it shows anything different, this could be the result of a number of problems, but may be an indicator of dashpod failure – an issue that plagued many TTs. If the car shows these symptoms, check with the seller whether the original dashpod (the instrument binnacle) has ever been replaced.

Check the steering is straight and the car doesn't pull to either side under braking. A clunky feel to the gearbox in first and second gears is typical of Audis, and no cause for concern.

Check that the heated seats are working.

Hidden in the compartment forward of the gear stick you will find switches for the fuel cap release, interior alarm sensor and boot release.

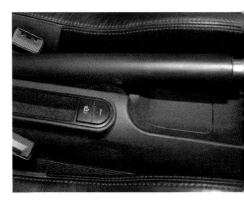

Next to the handbrake you will find switches for the door locks.

Now you've driven the car for a short while it's time to do that scan for ECU fault codes. Any faults shown may not necessarily mean major mechanical problems, and indeed as often as not are just issues with the sensors themselves, so don't let the appearance of one or two recorded faults be an immediate deal-breaker. Record what the fault codes are and seek some advice. Most Audi dealers or VAG independent specialists will be happy to give you general advice over the phone, though of course they'd need to see the car themselves before they could offer a firm diagnosis. You can also search for the codes on the internet to give you an indication of what the faults are. If the scan shows a host of recorded faults, that's a good indication that very little effort has been put into maintenance of the car, and its probably best to walk away. Always remember that intermittent faults may not have manifested during your short test drive, so even a clear scan at this stage does not ensure a complete absence of issues.

If you have completed your initial inspection and are still considering this car, then it's time to move on to a serious evaluation.

# 8 Key points
– where to look for problems

### VIN plate
This is a silver adhesive label situated in the engine bay on the left hand side as you look at it from the front. It will display the chassis number for the vehicle.

### Chassis number
This is stamped into the bulkhead to the rear of the engine bay. It is covered by the plastic scuttle at the base of the windscreen, but can be seen through a clear, plastic window.

### Dashboard display
There is a visible display of the chassis number on the left hand side of the dashboard, which can be seen through the windscreen from outside of the car.

### Engine number
On 1.8T models, the engine number is stamped into a machined area on the cylinder block casting near the oil filter flange. On 3.2 models the number is stamped into a machined area of the cylinder block at the back side near the connection between the engine and transmission. These are difficult to see.

### Build label
A paper label, usually in the spare wheel well, should also display the chassis number, engine code and paint code, together with a code identifying the interior fitted.

### Registration documents
Ensure the paperwork matches what is displayed on the car.

This build label in the spare wheel well provides information on the car's construction, including engine and paint codes.

The VIN plate on the right edge of the engine bay.

The chassis number is stamped into the bodyshell beneath this window in the scuttle.

You will also find the chassis number on the dashboard.

# 9 Serious evaluation
– 60 minutes for years of enjoyment

**Score each section as follows:**
4 = excellent; 3 = good; 2 = average; 1 = poor.
The totting up procedure is detailed at the end of the chapter. Be realistic in your marking!

### General exterior condition

4 3 2 1

Look for dents and scratches to the bodywork. Door dents caused by other cars in car parks are common, as are minor scrapes to the outer edges of the wheel arches. Also look for damage to the underside of the front spoiler from speed bumps. Check the condition of the front bumper and grilles and the forward edge of the bonnet, which tend to pick up stone-chip damage. This is also common on the wing mirrors.

The car may look good from a distance, but closer inspection can reveal stone chips to the front end.

### Paint

4 3 2 1

The paint used on TTs is usually of good quality and it is rare to see signs of bubbling or sub-surface corrosion. One place you may see wear is the rails that edge the roof above the doors. Some of these roof rails came out of the factory with faulty corrosion treatment, so bubbling can occur. On later cars it may be possible to have this rectified under the ten-year paint warranty, although in some cases the roof rails are interpreted by dealers as trim rather than bodywork, and they refuse the work.

Paint bubbling to the aluminium roof rails is a common fault. There is an inconsistent approach amongst dealers to warranty repair.
(Courtesy John Handford)

If not washed with care, swirls can appear on the surface of the paint. Audi do apply a decent thickness of paint, so it is possible to rectify minor surface scratches by machine polishing. The recesses behind the door handles can be prone to scratches, and it is difficult to get a polisher in there, so excessive damage here can be trickier to rectify.

### Panels

4 3 2 1

Panel fit from the factory is invariably excellent. Gaps between panels should be narrow and even. The static panels all fit very closely. Look for any uneven gaps that may indicate poor accident repairs or panels which have been removed and refitted badly. Corrosion is unusual and is generally only a result of poorly executed

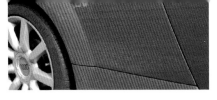

repairs or paint damage that has been left unrepaired for prolonged periods. Around the wheel arches, and the edges of the panels where the lower sill meets the rear three-quarter panel between the door and the rear wheelarch, are the most common areas where you may see paint bubbling.

This area of the car often picks up minor accident damage. Look for signs of poorly executed repairs.

## Shut lines

4 3 2 1

The key horizontal line of the car runs from the lower edge of the side of the bonnet, over the front wheelarch, along the door, through the handle, and then drops over the rear wheelarch. Check this line runs straight through the door. Misalignment can indicate accident damage or a poorly fitted door. The weight of the door can cause the hinges to slip over time, so these may simply need re-adjusting. Open the door and look for worn paint on the back edge inside the door shut. Again, this can indicate a badly fitted door but could also arise from the door cards having been removed and the rubber seals not being refitted properly.

Sight down the side of the car, checking panel fit and shut lines and looking for dents. (Courtesy Josh Dennison)

Wear on the door shut can arise either from a poorly fitted door card or misaligned door.

## Exterior trim

4 3 2 1

As previously mentioned, the plastics of the front grilles can pick up stone-chip damage, so check the condition of these. The grilles on most models are bare plastic, but those on the Quattro Sport should be painted gloss black. Check the scuttle at the base of the windscreen to ensure it is fitted correctly. Check the rubbers around the side windows for poor fitting or damage.

## Wipers

There are two styles of wipers fitted to the TT, depending on its age. Earlier cars were fitted with the more traditional wipers and arms, while from 2002 onwards low profile aero wipers were fitted. Check they are working and positioned correctly when not in use. Make sure they clear the screen effectively.

Aero wipers were fitted to post-2002 cars. Check the condition of the wipers and ensure they clear the screen properly.

## Soft top

Check the general condition of the fabric, looking for tears and abrasions. In particular, check for damage in the crease lines, created when the top is folded away. Look for damage to the rear window. Check front catches secure the roof to the top of the screen properly, and that the motor to lower and raise the roof functions correctly. Also check that the glass wind deflector operates correctly. The switches for both the roof and deflector are located behind the handbrake. Make sure the car has its softtop cover (to be fitted over the roof when it is folded down), which should be stored in the boot.

Ensure the wind deflector operates and the roof catches at the top of the windscreen secure properly. (Courtesy Iain Manson)

## Glass

Check the windscreen for stone-chips and all windows for scratches that may have been sustained from poor cleaning. Don't forget to include the wing mirrors. These are heated and come on automatically when the ignition is turned on. Check the heating elements in these and the rear window are working.

## Lights

The TT is fitted with HID xenon lights. If either is not working, it may just be a bulb. However, it could be an issue with the ballasts, which limit the electrical current

Look closely at the light cluster for signs of moisture and condensation within.

This fine rod is part of the headlight self-levelling system – it can break.

delivered to the lights to stop them overheating, and these can be expensive to replace. The regulations of most countries require HID lights to be accompanied by a washing system. The TT has a pair of wash jets fitted within the bumper under the light cluster. These will operate when you activate the windscreen wash while the lights are switched on. Check that these are working properly. Misting can occur within the light units if the seals degrade, so look for signs of condensation. The lights also have a self-levelling system. This is controlled by fine rods connected to the left-hand side of both the rear and front suspension assemblies, and they can often break. This would be a failure point for most road-worthiness tests, so check that those rods are intact.

## Tyres

4  3  2  1

The quattro drive system is not best utilised unless good quality tyres are fitted all-round, and mismatched tyres also fail to make the most of the drive system. Ideally, the car should be fitted with four identical tyres in similar condition. It makes little sense to fit budget tyres, and good quality replacements are expensive, so check the condition of those fitted, checking tread depth and wear patterns. Front tyres should wear slightly more than the rears, but rotating the wheels can extend their life. Noticeable disparity in wear between front and rear tyres indicates this hasn't been done by the current owner.

Uneven wear of the tyres can indicate a number of issues. Greater wear to the inside edges of the rear tyres can indicate excessive camber to the wheels. This is common when the car has been lowered with an aftermarket suspension and the additional camber created has not been adjusted by also fitting adjustable tie-bars. Excessive wear to the outer edges of the front tyres indicates too much toe-in and wheel alignment issues. Look for damage to the side walls.

Uneven wear can be seen on the inside edge of this tyre – a common sign of excess camber.

## Wheels

4  3  2  1

The TT is fitted with alloy wheels as standard. Some minor kerb scratches may be expected, but look for any more serious damage that may indicate a more substantial impact. When driving the car check for vibration in the steering, as this could indicate a buckled wheel. A choice of wheels was available as

An exclusive wheel design was fitted to the QS model. (Courtesy Scott Isherwood)

original equipment on most models, though the QS came with an exclusive design. If you want your car to be entirely original, a search on the internet should tell you which wheels should be fitted to the car you are looking at.

Many may be fitted with aftermarket replica wheels. These may be of a lower standard of construction, using less robust materials, and therefore more prone to damage. When removing the wheels to check other components, look for original Audi part numbers stamped on the inside surface.

Most original wheels have caps to cover the wheel bolts, which are often lost, so check that all four are fitted. Locking wheel nuts were factory-fitted. Make sure the key for these is present – it should be stored with the spare wheel.

## Seats

Check leather condition for wear: the outer bolster of the driver's seat is most

prone to scuffing. Check the seat adjustment: front and back lateral movement is adjusted with the lever to the front and towards the centre tunnel of the car. The backs tilt forward, released by levers either side of the seat which are positioned near the hinge. The angle of the seat backs is adjusted by turning a knob on the outer side, at the hinge. The driver's seat is height adjustable with the lever positioned to the side of the seat on the door side. Note the Recaro seats fitted in the QS have only front and back lateral adjustment.

In most models the seats are heated. Heating elements can fail if the wires are damaged, breaking the circuit. The controls are found on the dashboard (the two outermost of the five controls to the centre of the dash). Pressing the control will cause the dial to pop out, and rotating it clockwise will switch on the heating elements. Red LED lights should appear around the dial to indicate the heat level. You should feel the seats warming up within a minute or two.

Wear to the outside bolster of the driver's seat is common. Does it appear consistent with the claimed mileage of the car?

Check the rear seats fold down correctly, released by catches on the back which are accessed by opening the tailgate. Look for signs of damage to the back of the seats caused by loads in the boot.

## Seat belts

Inertia reel seatbelts are fitted both front and back. For all four belts ensure the inertia mechanisms engage with a sharp pull on the belt, and check the buckles

Check the entire length of all seatbelts for signs of fraying or tears.

secure and release correctly. Check the belts themselves for signs of wear or damage, pulling them out as far as they will go to examine the full length of the belt.

## Carpets

4  3  2  1

The carpets are durable, and suffer little wear due to the standard footwell mats, which have a stud fixing system to hold them in place. If the mats in the car are worn replacements are readily available, either as OEM equipment from Audi, or good aftermarket versions. Ingress of water is a common problem with many VAG vehicles using this chassis, and is usually a result of water collecting in the doors due to a failure of the internal seals, or as a result of the drainage holes to the underside of the door getting blocked. Check the carpets for any signs of dampness or water stains that would suggest this issue.

## Headlining

4  3  2  1

Though uncommon, look for minor tears or marks in the headlining. Replacing the lining is rather difficult, so to achieve a tidy and smooth finish, you will likely need a professional fitter. Pay attention to the areas around the tailgate opening, where damage is most likely to occur.

Tears in the lining and trim can often be found around the edges of the boot.

## Door cards & interior panels

4  3  2  1

The lower sections of the door panels can get scuffed when getting into the car if access is restricted. Also look for damage to the storage nets. The brushed aluminium of the door handles picks up scratches, as do the discs at the lower end of the grab handles. The screw that holds on the door cards is behind those discs, and where the door cards have been removed it is common for

The lower edges of the door cards can become scuffed. This car is fitted with a Bose sound system.

the catch that holds the disc in place to have been damaged, resulting in them occasionally dropping off, so check they are secure. Look for scratches to the dash and other panels. The textured surface of these makes scratches almost impossible to repair, so significant damage would need a replacement panel to sort out. Also look at the contact points of the storage compartments, especially the sliding lid of the compartment forward of the gearlever. Regular use is inevitable to access the boot and fuel cap releases, and this tends to wear away the rubberised surface, exposing the shiny plastic underneath. Again, this cannot be repaired, and a new panel would be needed.

### Door locks

Ensure the central locking functions correctly on both doors using the remote key. There is also a manual locking button located next to the handbrake. You may have seen when opening the doors the windows drop slightly, rising again when the door is shut to create an effective seal around the frameless windows. This is controlled by a micro-switch in the door lock, which does get worn out and can often fail. Make sure the windows function properly when the door is opened and closed.

The remote release for the tailgate is one of the three switches located in the compartment forward of the gear stick. Check that it works. There is also a micro-switch in that lock mechanism which controls the interior light for the boot. If the light does not come on the switch may be faulty, although quite often all that is required is a bit of cleaning.

### Window switches

The window switches are behind the door grab handles at the base: a double switch for both windows on the driver's side, and a single switch on the passenger's side. A quick touch and release on all of these switches should lower or raise the windows fully. Pressing and holding the switch will operate the windows until the switch is released. If these are not functioning correctly, it may just be a glitch in the control unit that can be reset manually. With the ignition switched on, lower the window all the way and then raise it all the way up, letting go of the switch once the window is fully closed. Press and hold the switch in the up position for five seconds, release it, and turn the ignition off. If the windows are still not functioning as they

The window switches are tucked neatly behind the door grab handle.

should on turning the ignition back on, the issue will be with either the switches or the winder motor.

The windows have an auto-close function, and should close themselves if left open when the doors are locked with the remote key.

### Steering wheel

The steering wheel is either leather or alcantara (standard for the QS). A well-used wheel will be smooth and shiny. Check that the general wear of the steering wheel appears consistent with the claimed mileage of the car.

When driving, ensure the wheel is centred correctly – it can't be fitted offset as there are sensors linked with the ESP system to detect steering angle, so if the wheel is not perfectly centred when driving straight, it indicates wheel alignment issues.

## Instrument panel & dashboard ☐4 ☐3 ☐2 ☐1

Dashpod failure is a notoriously common fault on the TT, with media campaigns taking place in both the UK and USA to get Audi to acknowledge the fault and offer replacements. There was never a recall however, with Audi agreeing to replace faulty dashpods as a goodwill gesture as-and-when failures occur. Many have been replaced, but not all. Failures manifest mostly as false readings from either of the fuel or temperature gauges, though dashpod failure is not the only cause behind these symptoms. The fuel gauge reading can be compared with the range shown on the driver information system. The range can vary considerably, depending on how vigorously the car has been driven recently, but generally a full tank will deliver between 300-400 miles. Check that the indicated range is compatible with the fuel gauge reading.

The temperature gauge should rise to 90°C and then remain there. If it shows a different reading it could be a sensor fault, a faulty thermostat, or could indicate dashpod failure. The sensor reading can be checked using the display of the air-conditioning unit. Press the 'recycle' and 'up' buttons together. The display will change to '1C.' Twist the temperature control until the display shows '49C.' Now press the 'recycle' button once more, and the display will show the actual coolant temperature measured by the sensor. (Pressing 'recycle' and 'up' together once more returns the air conditioner control back to its normal function). The actual

The AC unit can be used to access readings from various sensors on the car.

temperature reading should be within the 80-105°C range. If the actual temperature reading sits within that range, but the dashpod is showing something significantly different, then dashpod failure is likely. If the temperature reading shown via the air-conditioning unit is outside the 80-105°C range and corresponding with the dashpod then a faulty thermostat is most likely.

Faults can also occur with the LED display of the Driver Information System, which appears as horizontal lines either missing through the display or permanently displayed.

It may still be possible to get the dashpod replaced by Audi, though different conditions need to be met in different markets, so check with your local Audi dealer. If you cannot get a free replacement new units are expensive, though repair services to rectify faulty dashpods are available.

## Boot interior ☐4 ☐3 ☐2 ☐1

The TT is blessed with a large and useable boot, so it can see more service than those of other sports cars. Check the linings for tears and other damage, paying attention to the backs of the rear seats. See that the folding cover for the spare wheel well is in one piece and opens correctly with its handle undamaged. There are rings at the four corners for a cargo net – ensure these are in place. A cargo net itself was an optional accessory, so you may not find one with the car. Check the rubber seals around the boot for any tears. The tailgate itself is very heavy but should open easily, supported by two hydraulic struts. Check these for signs of oil leaks. If the tailgate is hard to lift those struts may have leaked in the past and may need replacing. Make sure the light to the left of the boot comes on when the tailgate is lifted.

## Spare wheel & tool kit

Where a spare is supplied, it is a space-saver wheel. Make sure it is there and in good condition. The tool kit is stored above the wheel. This should include a jack, wheel brace, towing eye, wheel locknut, plastic wheel locating rod, spanner, screwdriver, finger hook for wheel centre caps, and a plastic ground sheet. The V6 and Quattro Sport have no spare wheel, but instead come with a foam tyre inflator canister. There should be a warning triangle stored in a red box attached to the back of the boot. Check that everything is there.

Check that the car has a spare wheel (where supplied), and the tool kit is complete.

## VIN & data plates

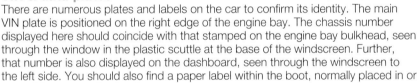

There are numerous plates and labels on the car to confirm its identity. The main VIN plate is positioned on the right edge of the engine bay. The chassis number displayed here should coincide with that stamped on the engine bay bulkhead, seen through the window in the plastic scuttle at the base of the windscreen. Further, that number is also displayed on the dashboard, seen through the windscreen to the left side. You should also find a paper label within the boot, normally placed in or around the spare wheel well.

Check these show the same number, but also that there are no signs that they have ever been removed or altered. The main VIN plate is an adhesive label and the edges should be even and flat. If there is any distortion it's a sure sign it has at some time been removed from the car and may indeed come from a different car altogether. If you have any doubts, remove the scuttle to check the stamped number and see if there are signs of alteration, or if a plate has been inserted under the scuttle.

## Turbo boost circuit

Naturally, you will not find a turbo on a 3.2 V6.

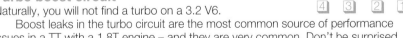

Boost leaks in the turbo circuit are the most common source of performance issues in a TT with a 1.8T engine – and they are very common. Don't be surprised to find leaks apparent in anything but the very best maintained cars. They occur either from splits in hoses or due to loose connections.

By removing the plastic cover to the top of the engine you will expose access to a host of hoses. If you are familiar with how a turbo system works, you should be

able to identify the main hoses. As you look at the engine bay from the front of the car, the turbo is situated centrally behind the engine. The turbo intake pipe branches off to your right, leading to the air filter box. The charge pipe is the L-shaped metal tube to the left of the bay. If you're not familiar with how a turbo works then a reasonable rule of thumb is that the larger hoses you see are generally associated with the turbo system. Squeeze these hoses and release them. Look for any splits as you squeeze, and check that they quickly regain their shape. Hoses that are split or tend to stick together when released are at the end of their life and will need replacing. Replacement silicone hoses may have been fitted to the car, and these shouldn't compress easily at all.

When test-driving the car the turbo should produce a whistling sound as it spools-up under acceleration, rather than hissing – this would indicate a leak somewhere. It does take a practiced ear to discern the difference.

## Diverter valve

The turbo system also needs a diverter valve (DV). The turbine within the turbo spins independently of the engine, driven by exhaust gasses which are forced through it. The rotation of the turbine then forces boost gases into the engine, the flow of which is controlled by the throttle body. When the throttle is released that flow of boost gasses is interrupted. If there was nowhere for that gas to go the build-up of pressure within the turbo loop would stop the turbine rotating, but ideally the turbine needs to keep spinning ready to provide boost gasses once the throttle is engaged again. Therefore, there is a DV to release gasses from the system

The standard diverter valve. It should emit an even hiss when the throttle is released.

when your foot is off the gas pedal. If not serviced this valve can start to stick, affecting performance. The DV is located to the back of the engine bay, above the turbo. The standard unit is made of black plastic, but many cars may be fitted with an improved version milled from billeted aluminium. When releasing the throttle this should produce an even hiss, rather than a fluttering noise which will indicate either it is sticking or there is a vacuum leak in the hoses leading to the valve.

## Turbo wear & oil leaks

The turbo is lubricated with oil from the engine. When the engine is switched off that flow of oil stops, but the turbine may continue to spin, as it rotates quite independently. As it spins at an extremely high rate, the turbine gets very hot, so it's important to leave the engine running for a short time after coming to rest – this keeps the oil flowing over the turbine, helping it to cool. Failing to do so allows the oil to become static around the turbine and the intense heat will burn the oil away. When the car is started again the lack of lubrication results in wear to the turbo which, if repeated regularly, can produce oil leaks in the system. There are two ways to detect this. First look for signs of blue smoke coming from the exhaust when starting the engine from cold. Otherwise disconnect the upper boost hose that leads into the throttle body attached to the inlet manifold at the front of the engine (on the right of the manifold for 225s or QS and the left for other cars). Some traces of oil are normal here, but signs of excessive oil in this hose indicate leaks in the turbo.

## Oil

The engine does burn oil and needs topping-up every 1000 miles or so. Check the oil levels; if they are low that may be an indication the previous owner hasn't been keeping on top of this. The oil should appear clear rather than black. Open the oil filler cap. Signs of a white mayonnaise-like substance around the filler could indicate a failure of the cylinder head gasket, however this can also appear on low mileage cars that have only ever done infrequent, short journeys, without there being any actual faults. Look at the underside of the filler cap. Traces of a dark, tar-like substance indicate the wrong oil has been used, or that changes have been too infrequent.

Check the oil filler cap for either a white, mayonnaise-like substance or dark tar deposits.

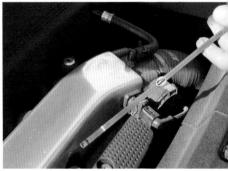

The oil should appear clear and not black.

### Injector seals

On a 1.8T engine the four fuel injectors are located on top of the manifold to the front of the engine. Look for signs of oil on the manifold around the base of the injectors, which indicates a failure of the seals. These will need to be replaced if leaking.

Stains like this on the inlet manifold indicate a failed injector seal.

## Pipework

4  3  2  1

Carry out a squeeze test on the rest of the pipework around the engine. Again, once released the tubes should quickly regain their shape. If not, the rubber is perishing and the pipes will need replacing sooner rather than later. Look for splits, tears or other signs of leaks, and check the connections are secure.

Squeeze and release the hoses. They should regain shape quickly and not stick together.

The vacuum hose at the end of the inlet manifold frequently splits. More durable silicone replacements are available.

## Brakes

4  3  2  1

The brake pedal should feel firm and engage without excessive travel. If the brakes feel spongy, this could indicate issues with the brake fluid, which would need to be drained and replaced.
The car is fitted with a brake wear indicator which appears on the dash as concentric yellow circles with an exclamation mark in the centre. Check the discs for signs of scoring or lips to the edges. Also check for corrosion, especially on a car that may not have been driven for some time. Light corrosion to the circumference of the discs is quite normal.

Look for scoring and rust on the brake discs. Rust around the edges is normal and quite acceptable.

On the test drive find somewhere safe to test the brakes. Braking firmly (rather than an emergency stop), check for any feel of juddering, which can arise from warped discs. The car should slow smoothly and remain straight, with the majority of the braking occurring on the front wheels. Pulling to either side can indicate uneven braking and an issue with one of the callipers. An emergency stop or braking on a wet or poor road surface is likely to activate the ABS system, resulting in characteristic pulse braking.

## Clutch

4  3  2  1

The clutch, with a dual-mass flywheel, is an expensive replacement. It tends to be

good for 100,000 miles, though many are still running well long after that. With a vigorous take-off from a standing start, feel for any signs of juddering which would suggest a worn flywheel. To test the clutch plates, accelerate hard in third gear. Any slippage should be detected as a break in power delivery at around 3500rpm.

There have been issues with clutch pedals fracturing. Using a mirror, check the back of the pedal for signs of any cracks.

## Trackrod ends

These connections get worn over time. With the engine running to enable power steering and with the wheels on the ground, rock the steering gently from side to side. Listen for any knocking noise betraying wear in the trackrod ends.

## Ball joints

There is much to check under the car, so if you can get it to a garage with a hoist that would be ideal. Failing that, jacking the car onto stands will suffice. Take care that the stands are properly placed, that you position blocks under the wheels in case any of the stands fail, and take great care whilst under the car. If you can't get the car off the ground check what you can: a mirror on a long handle will prove useful for this.

One item to check that does need the wheels off the ground are the ball joints which connect the lower wishbone arms to the wheel hubs. With the car jacked-up, manipulate the wheels by hand to feel for any play. These do get worn, so any movement can suggest the ball joints need replacing.

## Coil springs

The suspension on Audis tends to be rather firm, so doesn't give much when hitting potholes or obstructions on the road surface – hence cracked or broken springs are not uncommon. They tend to break towards the ends, so the coils will remain held in place by the weight of the car even though they won't function properly. Getting the car off the ground should make any damage obvious, but if you are unable to do that examine the springs as closely as you can with a mirror, paying particular attention to where the springs are seated at the top.

*If the springs crack or break it is usually near the ends of the coils. Getting the car off its wheels makes damage easier to detect.*

## CV boots

There are constant velocity (CV) joints at the ends of each of the drive shafts connecting the shafts to the wheels. Each of these CV joints is protected with a corrugated, rubber-like plastic boot to prevent water ingress and damage to the

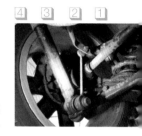

joints. These often split. Split boots are a failure point for most statutory roadworthiness tests so any that are damaged will need to be replaced.

## Drive shafts

Check the areas around the connections at each end of all drive shafts (whether your car has two or four) for signs of any oil leaks. Leaking oil from any of the joints will migrate along the shafts and attract and capture dirt, giving a dark staining to the shaft. Leaks indicate failed seals which will need to be replaced.

Look for oil on the drive shafts that could indicate a leak at the connections.

## Power steering lines

Any leaking fluid from the power steering can usually be detected by signs of oil on the engine under tray to the left-hand side of the car. Removal of the tray can be difficult, as the screws holding it in place often get corroded and attempts to unfasten them tend to shear them off, so don't try this without the seller's permission. Getting the tray off will reveal the lines for the power steering and help you locate the source of the leak, but if you are unable to do that mark it down and note it as something you will need to examine further if you buy the car.

Leaks in the power steering lines can often be spotted by signs of oil on this undertray.

## Wishbone bushes

Check the bushes pressed into the joints at the apex of the lower suspension wishbones. These will wear in time. In good condition, they should sit flush with the thin metal collar that surrounds them. As they wear out they tend to drop from the surrounds, leaving a lip. Also look for signs of perishing, indicated by small cracks in the bush itself.

The metal surround of the wishbone bushes should be flush with the bush.

## Drop link bushes

There are drop links on the rear suspension which are connected at the lower end

next to the bottom of the rear shock absorbers. These connections have bushes which can wear out. As the bushes wear the drop link tends to migrate towards the shock absorber. There should be a noticeable gap between the two, but if the drop link is settled against the shock absorber the bush is worn and will need replacing.

Look for the drop link being hard against the shock absorber, indicating the bush is worn and needs replacing.

## Strut mounts

The tops of the front suspension units sit in rubberised mounts and project through

into the engine bay, capped by plastic discs. When the mounts are in good order the discs should sit quite close to the surface of the engine bay. The mounts compress over time, resulting in the struts rising further into the engine bay. With the car on its wheels, check the gap between the plastic strut covers and the engine bay beneath. A broad gap indicates worn strut mounts.

Look for wide gaps under the strut caps. The mounts may be worn.

## Haldex

The Haldex is the unit that controls the distribution of drive power to each of the four wheels and is the heart of the quattro system (where fitted). The Haldex unit and its controller are positioned next to the rear differential, forward of the rear driveshaft coupling. Check around the unit for any signs of leaking oil.

The Haldex is the heart of the quattro drive system.

## Anti-roll bar bushes

Like all the other bushes, those fitted to the anti-roll bars become worn. The best way to diagnose wear in these is by driving the car over speed bumps, listening for a knocking sound.

The anti-roll bar connects to the top of the drop link, and the tie bar to the bottom of the hub. More bushes in these connections that can be worn out.

## Rear tie bars

Tie bars to the rear restrict the camber of the rear wheels. The bushes connecting the tie bars to the axles get worn which then allows the car to sink slightly, increasing camber. To check for this, look at the rear tyres for signs of excessive wear to the inside edges of the tread. Excessive camber can also occur when aftermarket suspension has been fitted to lower the car. The original equipment allows for only limited adjustment to correct the extra camber that will arise, so when lowering the car it is advisable to fit adjustable tie bars to correct the camber back into factory tolerances. Where the suspension has been lowered and the tie bars not replaced, you are likely to find signs of excessive wear to the inside edges of the rear tyres.

## Cambelt

The V6 has a timing chain which does not require routine maintenance, but the 1.8T engine is fitted with a cambelt. Depending on the age of the car, the official Audi service schedule recommends the cambelt be changed at anything up to 115,000 miles. However, experience has shown owners that there is a significant risk of cambelt failure at anything from 60,000 miles onwards – considerably less than the service schedule suggests. A belt

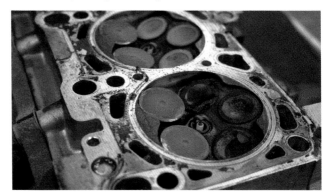

The aftermath of a cambelt failure. Bent valves and damage to the piston heads are the minimum to expect. It could be terminal.

failure is likely to cause serious damage to the engine and will be very expensive to repair. Unfortunately, the belt is not readily accessible, so a visual inspection of its condition is perhaps outside the scope of this sort of purchasing evaluation. It is important that you question the seller regarding the history of the car and whether the cambelt has been changed. If it has ask to see receipts for the work done. If the car has over 60,000 miles on the clock and there is no evidence that the cambelt has ever been changed then factor the cost of getting it done into your purchase price and get the belt changed immediately.

There is a hydraulic damper for the tensioner pulley that is not routinely part of a cambelt change described by the Audi service manuals, but again experience has shown this item can fail, resulting in expensive engine damage. If you are getting the work done, the damper should also be changed. It is also recommended that the water pump be replaced at the same time as the belt.

## Wiring & electrics

As we have seen there are a large number of electrical systems on the car, serviced by an extensive and complex wiring loom, and it can be very difficult for anyone other than a professional auto-electrician to find the source of faults or breakages in any of

The electric wiring around the engine is neatly contained in plastic sheathing.

The wiring in this conduit between the doors and bulkhead is well-protected but could suffer breakages.

the hundreds of wires involved. It is easier to check that the systems are all working correctly than comprehensively evaluate the condition of the wiring, however as you inspect the rest of the car pay attention to the visible wiring. Bundles of wires are generally wrapped in fabric tape or contained in plastic sheaths to protect them from the elements. Where tape is broken or removed or sheaths cut, you might expect to see evidence of repairs, or the addition of non-factory wiring. Poorly executed wiring connections for additional electrical items are a potential fire risk, so be wary of these.

Breaks in wiring are most common where the looms are frequently subjected to movement – for example where they connect to the doors and tailgate. If there are problems with the central locking, windows or interior lights, these may be a result of broken wires at that part of the loom. These sections of wiring are protected by corrugated hosing – the ends of which are simply pressed into the recesses of the body panels. They can easily be pulled free so the condition of the wires can be checked and then pressed back into place when done. However, damaged wires may not always be visible on a quick inspection.

The fuses are located at the end of the dash.

Of course, failed electrical systems may be a result of a simple blown fuse, though you'd expect a seller to resolve such issues prior to you examining the car. The fuse box is situated behind a panel at the right end of the dashboard, seen with the door open, and prised off gently with a screwdriver.

## Engines & engine identification
Earlier 1.8T cars (99-00) were fitted with APX code engines (AMU in the USA) and BAM code engines thereafter. The engine code should be indicated on the car's registration documents. There are some differences between these engines. The APX/AMU engines have a secondary air injection system, while the BAM engines operate with variable valve timing. The turbo systems also differ substantially, and many of the sensors associated with the turbo are specific to their engines. When ordering parts it is important to know which engine you have. In terms of function, the general consensus is that neither engine is particularly preferable over the other, so whether an AMU/APX or BAM engine is fitted has little influence on the value of the car.

This engine is the 1.8T as fitted to a QS.
Note the throttle body to the right of the
inlet manifold.

The well-presented V6 engine is instantly
recognisable.

As mentioned elsewhere the most obvious visual difference between the 225 engine and the lower powered versions is the inlet manifold to the front of the engine. On the 225 engines the throttle body is attached to the right, while it is on the left on the other engines. The QS has the same BAM engine as the later 225s, with no visible differences other than the relocation of the battery into the boot.

The 1.8T engine has proved itself to be very reliable, with serious issues tending to arise only from cambelt failures. The damage sustained from this is often serious enough to render a repair of the engine less economical than simply transplanting a complete, salvaged engine. If you find the car does not have its original engine, this is a likely cause.

Failures of the head gasket are uncommon but not unheard of. With the engine cover off, take a look around the engine block for any signs of oil leaks.

## Test drive (not less than 15 minutes)

To take the car for a test drive you will need to ensure appropriate insurance cover. Remember, you will be driving someone else's pride and joy, so take care while still giving the car a thorough test, and always have due consideration for other road users. Try and start the car from cold so you can see how it behaves as it warms up. It may be worth asking the seller to leave the car cold for you when making the viewing arrangements. If at all possible try and find a friendly garage nearby, who by prior arrangement, will allow you to use their hoist for a short time.

Some specifics for a test drive, with respect to testing the clutch, brakes, steering and aspects of the suspension, have already been covered. In general the car should feel tight and precise. It should drive straight, though as an essentially front-wheel drive car with ample power, some mild torque steer should be expected on acceleration. There shouldn't be any creaks or knocks over undulations or bumps.

## Evaluation procedure
Add up the total points.
**Score: 188 = excellent; 141 = good; 94 = average; 47 = poor.**
Cars scoring over 132 will be completely usable and will require only maintenance and care to preserve condition. Cars scoring between 47 and 96 will require some serious work (at much the same cost regardless of score). Cars scoring between 97 and 131 will require very careful assessment of the necessary repair/restoration costs in order to arrive at a realistic value.

# 10 Auctions
– sold! Another way to buy your dream

## Auction pros & cons
Pros
Prices will usually be lower than those of dealers or private sellers and you might grab a real bargain on the day except where there is high demand for a particular car. Auctioneers have usually established clear title with the seller. At the venue you can usually examine documentation relating to the vehicle.
Cons
You have to rely on a sketchy catalogue description of condition and history. The opportunity to inspect is limited and you cannot drive the car. Auction cars are often a little below par and may require some work. It's easy to overbid. There will usually be a buyer's premium to pay in addition to the auction hammer price.

## Which auction?
Auctions by established auctioneers are advertised in car magazines and on the auction houses' website. A catalogue, or a simple printed list of the lots for auctions might only be available a day or two ahead, though often lots are listed and pictured on auctioneers' websites much earlier. Contact the auction company to ask if previous auction selling prices are available as this is useful information (details of past sales are often available on websites).

## Catalogue, entry fee and payment details
When you purchase the catalogue of the vehicles in the auction it often acts as a ticket which allows two people to attend the viewing days and the auction itself. Catalogue details tend to be comparatively brief, but will include information such as 'one owner from new, low mileage, full service history,' etc. It will also usually show a guide price to give you some idea of what to expect to pay and will tell you what is charged as a 'Buyer's premium.' The catalogue will also contain details of acceptable forms of payment. At the fall of the hammer an immediate deposit is usually required, the balance payable within 24 hours. If the plan is to pay by cash there may be a cash limit. Some auctions will accept payment by debit card. Sometimes credit or charge cards are acceptable, but will often incur an extra charge. A bank draft or bank transfer will have to be arranged in advance with your own bank as well as with the auction house. No car will be released before all payments are cleared. If delays occur in payment transfers then storage costs can accrue.

## Buyer's premium
This will be added to the hammer price: don't forget this in your calculations. It is not usual for there to be a tax on the purchase price and/or on the buyer's premium.

## Viewing
In some instances it's possible to view on the day, or days before, as well as in the hours prior to the auction. There are auction officials available who are willing to help out by opening engine and luggage compartments and to allow you to inspect the interior. While the officials may start the engine for you, a test drive is out of the

question. Crawling under and around the car as much as you want is permitted, but you can't suggest that the car you are interested in be jacked-up, or attempt to do the job yourself. You can also ask to see any documentation available.

## Bidding

Before you take part in the auction, decide your maximum bid – and stick to it! It may take a while for the auctioneer to reach the lot you are interested in, so use that time to observe how other bidders behave. When it's the turn of your car, attract the auctioneer's attention and make an early bid. The auctioneer will then look to you for a reaction every time another bid is made, usually the bids will be in fixed increments until the bidding slows, when smaller increments will often be accepted before the hammer falls. If you want to withdraw from the bidding, make sure the auctioneer understands your intentions – a vigorous shake of the head when he or she looks to you for the next bid should do the trick. Assuming that you are the successful bidder, the auctioneer will note your card or paddle number, and from that moment on you will be responsible for the vehicle. If the car is unsold, either because it failed to reach the reserve or because there was little interest, it may be possible to negotiate with the owner, via the auctioneers, after the sale is over.

## Successful bid

There are two more items to think about. How to get the car home, and insurance. If you can't drive the car, your own or a hired trailer is one way, another is to have the vehicle shipped using the facilities of a local company. The auction house will also have details of companies specialising in the transfer of cars.

Insurance for immediate cover can usually be purchased on site, but it may be more cost-effective to make arrangements with your own insurance company in advance and then call to confirm the full details.

## eBay & other online auctions

eBay & other online auctions could land you a car at a bargain price, though you'd be foolhardy to bid without examining the car first, something most vendors encourage. A useful feature of eBay is that the geographical location of the car is shown, so you can narrow your choices to those within a realistic radius of home. Be prepared to be outbid in the last few moments of the auction. Remember, your bid is binding and that it will be very, very difficult to get restitution in the case of a crooked vendor fleecing you – caveat emptor!

Be aware that some cars offered for sale in online auctions are 'ghost' cars. Don't part with any cash without being sure that the vehicle does actually exist and is as described (usually pre-bidding inspection is possible).

## Auctioneers

Barons www.barons-auctions.com/ Barrett-Jackson www.barrett-jackson.com/ Bonhams www.bonhams.com/ British Car Auctions BCA) www.bca-europe.com or www.british-car-auctions.co.uk/ Cheffins www.cheffins.co.uk/ Christies www.christies.com/ Coys www.coys.co.uk/ eBay www.ebay.com/ H&H www.classic-auctions.co.uk/ RM www.rmauctions.com/ Shannons www.shannons.com.au/ Silver www.silverauctions.com

# 11 Paperwork
– correct documentation is essential!

## The paper trail
Classic, collector and prestige cars usually come with a large portfolio of paperwork accumulated and passed on by a succession of proud owners. This documentation represents the real history of the car and from it can be deduced the level of care the car has received, how much it's been used, which specialists have worked on it and the dates of major repairs and restorations. All of this information will be priceless to you as the new owner, so be very wary of cars with little paperwork to support their claimed history.

## Registration documents
All countries/states have some form of registration for private vehicles whether it's the American 'pink slip' system or the British 'log book' system.

It is essential to check that the registration document is genuine, that it relates to the car in question, and that all the vehicle's details are correctly recorded, including chassis/VIN/car and engine numbers (if these are shown). If you are buying from the previous owner, his or her name and address will be recorded in the document: this will not be the case if you are buying from a dealer.

In the UK the current (Euro-aligned) registration document is named 'V5C' and is printed in coloured sections of blue, green and pink. The blue section relates to the car specification, the green section has details of the new owner and the pink section is sent to the DVLA in the UK when the car is sold. A small section in yellow deals with selling the car within the motor trade.

In the UK the DVLA will provide details of earlier keepers of the vehicle upon payment of a small fee, and much can be learned in this way.

If the car has a foreign registration there may be expensive and time-consuming formalities to complete. Do you really want the hassle and maybe tax to pay?

## Roadworthiness certificate
Most country/state administrations require that vehicles are regularly tested to prove that they are safe to use on the public highway and do not produce excessive emissions. In the UK that test (the 'MoT') is carried out at approved testing stations, for a fee. In the USA the requirement varies, but most states insist on an emissions test every two years as a minimum, while the police are charged with pulling over unsafe-looking vehicles.

In the UK the test is required on an annual basis once a vehicle becomes three years old. Of particular relevance for older cars is that the certificate issued includes the mileage reading recorded at the test date and, therefore, becomes an independent record of that car's history.

A roadster with the roof down on a perfect sunny day.
(Courtesy Chantelle Harris)

Ask the seller if previous certificates are available. Without an MoT the vehicle should be trailered to its new home, unless you insist that a valid MoT is part of the deal. (Not such a bad idea this, as at least you will know the car was roadworthy on the day it was tested and you don't need to wait for the old certificate to expire before having the test done.)

## Road licence

The administration of every country/state charges some kind of tax for the use of its road system, the actual form of the 'road licence' and, how it is displayed, varying enormously country to country and state to state.

Whatever the form of the 'road licence', it must relate to the vehicle carrying it and must be present and valid if the car is to be driven on the public highway legally.

In the UK if a car is untaxed because it has not been used for a period of time, the owner has to inform the licensing authorities, otherwise the vehicle's date-related registration number will be lost and there will be a painful amount of paperwork to get it re-registered.

## Certificates of authenticity

For many makes of collectible car it is possible to get a certificate proving the age and authenticity (eg engine and chassis numbers, paint colour and trim) of a particular vehicle, these are sometimes called 'Heritage Certificates' and if the car comes with one of these it is a definite bonus.

If the car has been used in European classic car rallies it may have a FIVA (Federation Internationale des Vehicules Anciens) certificate. The so-called 'FIVA Passport', or 'FIVA Vehicle Identity Card,' enables organisers and participants to recognise whether or not a particular vehicle is suitable for individual events. If you want to obtain such a certificate go to www.fbhvc.co.uk or www.fiva.org there will be similar organisations in other countries too.

## Valuation certificate

Hopefully, the vendor will have a recent valuation certificate, or letter signed by a recognised expert stating how much he, or she, believes the particular car to be worth (such documents, together with photos, are usually needed to get 'agreed value' classic car insurance). Generally, such documents should act only as confirmation of your own assessment of the car rather than a guarantee of value, as the expert has probably not seen the car in the flesh. The easiest way to find out how to obtain a formal valuation is to contact the owners club.

## Service history

Often these cars will have been serviced at home by enthusiastic (and hopefully capable) owners for a good number of years. Nevertheless, try to obtain as much service history and other paperwork pertaining to the car as you can. Naturally, garage stamps or specialist garage receipts score most points in the value stakes. However, anything helps in the great authenticity game, items like the original bill of sale, handbook, parts invoices and repair bills, adding to the story and the character of the car. Even a brochure correct to the year of the car's manufacture is a useful document and something that you could well have to search hard to locate in future years. If the seller claims that the car has been restored, then expect receipts and other evidence from a specialist restorer.

If the seller claims to have carried out regular servicing, ask what work was completed, when, and seek some evidence of it being carried out. Your assessment of the car's overall condition should tell you whether the seller's claims are genuine.

## Restoration photographs

If the seller tells you that the car has been restored, then expect to be shown a series of photographs taken while the restoration was under way. Pictures taken at various stages, and from various angles, should help you gauge the thoroughness of the work. If you buy the car, ask if you can have all the photographs as they form an important part of the vehicle's history. It's surprising how many sellers are happy to part with their car and accept your cash, but want to hang on to their photographs! In the latter event, you may be able to persuade the vendor to get a set of copies made.

# 12 What's it worth?

– let your head rule your heart

## Desirable options/extras

Unlike many classic cars where there is a choice of body styles, the proponents of the TT coupé or roadster are just about equal, so the engine is far more likely to influence the desirability of the car. Having said that, the lower-powered 150 PS and 180 PS engine options are far more common in roadsters, and in some markets (such as the UK), the 150 PS engine was never offered in the coupé. While 225 PS coupés are plentiful, it is harder to find roadsters with that engine, so 225 roadsters will command a small premium.

The V6 and QS models have a more aggressive front end than the other versions.

The lightweight Recaro seats fitted to the QS won't suit everyone.

Rare colours are often sought-after, and some buyers will travel a long way to get the one they are looking for. (Courtesy Jonathan Clemens)

Unlike other derivatives, the 3.2 V6 was sold in fairly equal numbers as both coupé and roadster, so those who prefer the growl of a normally-aspirated V engine can enjoy a free choice in body styles, paying similar sums for each. These are also amongst the most recent examples of the car, and offer some minor bodywork modifications which are considered desirable. Further, because they are more powerful than the 225 PS 1.8T and less plentiful, you can expect to pay that bit more for one.

Naturally the Quattro Sport, having the best performance capabilities and being of limited edition, is the most sought-after example. It is, however, only available as a coupé, and the lack of rear seats and boot configuration present some practical limitations, so it doesn't suit everybody. Sadly, it was not sold in the US market.

There are some desirable factory options. There are a range of non-standard colours which were available through the Audi Exclusive Programme, and can make your TT stand out from the crowd. The baseball interior from the concept car was also offered in the roadster. Cruise control was only ever optional, though this can be easily and cheaply retrofitted using OEM parts. The BOSE sound system was an option in some models but standard in others, and is commonly found. A much less desirable option was Audi's satellite navigation system, which did not work very well and is rarely seen.

Optional extras, such as cruise control, are worth looking out for.

Modifications are common, especially if you buy from an enthusiast. The 1.8T engine can easily be tuned with negligible reliability issues, so many cars will have been remapped. This can typically add 30-40bhp, which makes an appreciable difference to the car's performance, but does have implications for obtaining insurance. Coupled with a remap, you will often find a replacement air-intake filter or aftermarket induction units, and upgraded DV and silicone turbo hoses. Buying a car with this work already done may save you the expense of having it done yourself. Suspension modifications are also common, with lowered springs or adjustable coilover units being fitted. These are much more a matter of personal preference, and are just as likely to reduce the value of a car as enhance it.

Modified cars won't be for everyone, but if the work has been done well they need not mean trouble. (Courtesy David Tonks)

# 13. Do you really want to restore?
– it'll take longer and cost more than you think

Still classed as a modern classic, most TTs are not particularly old. In addition, as mentioned elsewhere, a predominantly galvanised steel and aluminium body means that corrosion is not a major issue. That is not to say that older, higher mileage examples won't be starting to look a little tired. This presents an opportunity to buy a car more cheaply, and give you a chance to put some effort in to bring your car back to its former splendour without any major worries that your chosen project is irrecoverable.

One sizeable exception to this is, of course, crash-damaged vehicles. Major impacts resulting in distortion to the chassis frame are almost impossible to repair satisfactorily. With the engine mounted forward of the front axle, a substantial front-end impact is likely to have caused major damage that will be expensive to repair. As a result, insurance write-offs are exactly that, and are really only suitable to be broken down for spares. With so many roadworthy examples still out there we are perhaps still a decade or more away from a major restoration being a sensible proposition.

But, as stated, there can be great satisfaction gained from taking a tired and tatty TT and returning it to showroom condition. All original parts are still available from Audi dealerships, and many can be sourced via independent factors. In addition, there is a very healthy aftermarket tuning industry, originally built around the related VW Golf GTI, which readily lends its expertise to the Audi TT.

The factory paintwork is of an excellent quality and thickness, which allows corrective work to remove scratches and swirls. This can be a time-consuming, but ultimately very rewarding, process which can have remarkable results. With the right equipment and a small amount of instruction or research, it is a job within the capabilities of most.

Work on the suspension can also pay dividends in higher mileage cars. In time, the bushes on the linkages inevitably wear, which compromises the handling of the car and gives the steering a vague

Major work, such as fitting a turbo to this V6, can be expensive – but equally rewarding. (Courtesy Steve Collier)

feel. Replacing the bushes throughout makes a substantial difference, but this is a job which needs access to garage facilities with a hoist. A full wheel alignment is required once any work is done involving dismantling suspension elements, so it can be more cost-effective to get all the bushes replaced at the same time.

Hoses within the engine bay perish and split with time, resulting in boost leaks from the turbo system, so this is another area where restoration work can make great improvements. OEM hoses are of good quality, though when replacing them many choose to use more rigid and durable silicone examples. These are less prone to leaks and maintain their shape better, improving airflow through the system. Access to some hoses is difficult, though.

Relatively modest sums spent dressing the engine bay can produce great results.

# 14 Paint problems

– bad complexion, including dimples, pimples and bubbles

Paint faults generally occur due lack of protection/maintenance, or to poor preparation prior to a respray or touch-up. Some of the following conditions may be present in the car you're looking at:

## Orange peel
This appears as an uneven paint surface, similar to the appearance of the skin of an orange. The fault is caused by the failure of atomized paint droplets to flow into each other when they hit the surface. It's sometimes possible to rub out the effect with proprietory paint cutting/rubbing compound or very fine grades of abrasive paper. A respray may be necessary in severe cases. Consult a bodywork repairer/paint shop for advice on the particular car.

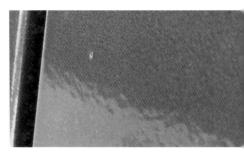

You may be able to rub out orange peel, but in severe cases a respray may be required..

## Cracking
Severe cases are likely to have been caused by too heavy an application of paint (or filler beneath the paint). Also, insufficient stirring of the paint before application can lead to the components being improperly mixed, and cracking can result. Incompatibility with the paint already on the panel can have a similar effect. To rectify the problem it is necessary to rub down to a smooth, sound finish before respraying the problem area.

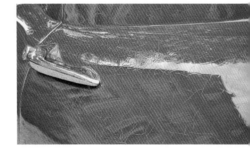

## Crazing
Sometimes the paint takes on a crazed rather than a cracked appearance when the problems mentioned under 'Cracking' are present. This problem can also be caused by a reaction between the underlying surface and the paint. Paint removal and respraying the problem area is usually the only solution.

When does cracking become crazing? Both will require paint removal and respraying.

## Blistering
Almost always caused by corrosion of the metal beneath the paint. Usually perforation will be found in the metal and the damage will usually be worse than that suggested by the area of blistering. The metal will have to be repaired before repainting.

## Micro blistering

Usually the result of an economy respray where inadequate heating has allowed moisture to settle on the car before spraying. Consult a paint specialist, but usually damaged paint will have to be removed before partial or full respraying. Micro blistering can also be caused by car covers that don't 'breathe.'

Blistering is almost always caused by corroded metal beneath the paint.

## Fading

Some colours, especially reds, are prone to fading if subjected to strong sunlight for long periods without the benefit of polish protection. Sometimes proprietary paint restorers and/or paint cutting/rubbing compounds will retrieve the situation. Often a respray is the only real solution.

## Peeling

Often a problem with metallic paintwork when the sealing lacquer becomes damaged and begins to peel off. Poorly applied paint may also peel. The remedy is to strip and start again!

## Dimples

Dimples in the paintwork are caused by the residue of polish (particularly silicone types) not being removed properly before respraying. Paint removal and repainting is the only solution.

## Dents

Small dents are usually easily cured by the 'Dentmaster,' or equivalent process, that sucks or pushes out the dent (as long as the paint surface is still intact). Companies offering dent removal services usually come to your home: consult your telephone directory.

# 15 Problems due to lack of use

– just like their owners, TTs need exercise!

All vehicles, if not used regularly, can develop problems, and the TT is no exception.

Common glycol ether-based brake fluid is hygroscopic, which means it can absorb water from the surrounding environment or atmosphere. This has a detrimental effect on the boiling point of the fluid and can cause corrosion within the braking system and its components, which is why it is a good idea to renew the brake fluid periodically, or if repairs are required. Modern silicone-based (DOT-5) brake fluids are hydrophobic and repel water, however the specification recommended for the TT is DOT-4 Super.

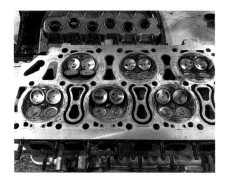

A V6 engine being stripped for work.
(Courtesy Steve Collier)

Brake calliper pistons can seize or stick in their bores if left for a long period of time, particularly if the braking system has the aforementioned glycol ether-based brake fluid.

Parking brake or emergency brake cables and mechanisms can seize if not well lubricated. This is particularly common on cars equipped with automatic transmissions, as many drivers rely on the parking pawl within the transmission only.

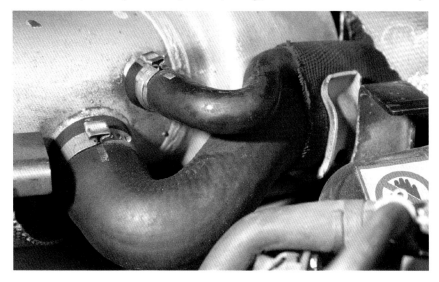

Turbo hoses can crack and perish. These appear to be in good condition.

Electrical contacts, if exposed to high humidity, can suffer from corrosion, leading to poor contacts and potentially non-functioning circuits. Given the numerous sensors fitted to the TT's various systems, this could result in issues with anything from the engine management to the ABS and drive systems.

Fuel systems can also be a problem area. If moisture or condensation forms inside the fuel tank, this could result in the fuel pickup drawing the water from the bottom of the tank (gasoline floats on water), and supplying this to the engine instead of gasoline. Fuel can also go stale – a problem aggravated by the increase of additives such as ethanol being blended in modern fuels with the intention of improving the octane rating.

Oil or grease is normally used to prevent metal-to-metal contact, such as the thin film of oil between the drive shafts and main bearing shells. If left for prolonged periods without use or rotation the oil can drain away from these parts, leaving them potentially exposed to moisture and corrosion. Regular use is the only real preventative.

Rubber components such as hoses can perish and crack, making them unsafe under high pressure – or worse, they can develop leaks. This is especially important to check on flexible brake hoses and within the fuel system. It can also be critical in the turbo boost circuit where leaks – though not dangerous – will have a detrimental effect on the performance of the car.

Tyres can develop flat spots if the vehicle is left standing in the same position for a long time. Similarly, the rubber can begin to perish, and cracks can develop in the sidewall and tread areas. This is especially common if the car is left outside and exposed to the sun's UV rays.

Automatic transmissions, if left standing for a long time, can suffer from leaks as a result of fluid draining back into the main case. The DSG gearbox has both a drain plug and a check plug located on the underside, and over time the seals can fail, leaving a puddle of oil on the driveway or garage floor.

Corrosion can be expected on some mechanical elements.

# 16 The Community
– key people, organisations and companies in the TT world

There are clubs throughout the world for TT enthusiasts.
(Courtesy Iain Manson)

## Clubs and websites
The enthusiasm that exists for the Audi TT has inevitably resulted in the creation of owners' clubs around the world. Many of these clubs are very active, staging events of their own, organising stands at various regional car shows and co-ordinating local groups, holding regular meetings, cruises or holidays. All have internet forums where owners can get support and expert advice. There are good working relationships between clubs in different countries around Europe, and trips to visit neighbouring countries and their clubs are organised regularly.

TT Owners' club (UK)
www.ttoc.co.uk

The TT forum (UK)
www.ttforum.co.uk

TT Car Club America
www.audittcca.org

Audi Club of North America
www.audiclubna.org

Southern California Audi TT Club
www.socalttclub.org

Audi Forum (Canada)
www.audiforum.ca

Clan TT (France)
www.clan-tt.com

TT Owners' club (Germany)
www.tt-owners-club.net

Audi TT Club (Italy)
www.audittclub.it

Audi TT Club (Spain)
www.audittclub.com

Audi TT Club (Netherlands)
www.audittclub.nl

Audi Owners' club
www.audiownersclub.com

## Specialists
VAG specialist retailers and garages are plentiful around the world. Many will have originated from tuning and modifying Golf GTIs and will be able to lend that expertise to the TT and other VAG cars. Some specialise in the TT itself, providing mechanical and tuning services, or retailing TT specific parts and accessories. All operate online retailing so you should have little difficulty finding the parts to tune and style your car to your specific needs.

The TT Shop
www.thettshop.com

Awesome GTi
www.awesomegti.com

JBS Autodesigns
www.jbsautodesigns.co.uk

Wak's Wide Web
www.wak-tt.com

APR Motorsport
www.goapr.co.uk

TT Stuff
www.ttstuff.com

GTT
www.gtt.uk.com

A TT being put through its paces on a track day. (Courtesy Jorge Enrique)

## Motorsport

There is little organised motorsport specific to the Audi TT, but the tuning possibilities of the engine make it a popular track day car that can be prepared and maintained at relatively modest expense. Most circuits operate open track days so you're almost certain to find a track near you where you can test the capabilities of yourself and your car. If you do use your car on a track day, remember that you're likely to be pushing the limits, which you may well cross. Accidents are sadly common and your regular insurance will not cover this sort of use. You can obtain specific trackday cover on a daily basis, which is highly recommended and on some tracks is compulsory.

## Books and magazines

The UK TTOC produce an excellent quarterly magazine *absoluTTe* which is distributed to club members, either as a printed, glossy magazine or as a web issue. Back-issues are available through the shop on the club website.

*Audi Driver Magazine* (www.audidrivermag.co.uk) covers all aspects of Audi ownership. In addition, *Audi Magazine* (www.audi-magazine.co.uk) is sent out by Audi to customers using its dealerships.

The definitive guide to maintaining and servicing your TT is the *Bentley Service Manual* from Bentley Publishers (www.bentleypublishers.com). This is available either in print or as a download.

TTOC members enjoying a beach barbecue.

# 17 Vital statistics

– essential data at your fingertips

| General | 1.8T | 3.2 V6 |
|---|---|---|
| Wheelbase/track front/track rear (mm) | 2422/1528/1513 | 2429/1528/1505 |
| Length/width/height (mm) | 4041/1764/1346 | 4041/1764/1348 |
| Drag coefficient | 0.32 | 0.35 |

| | FWD | 4WD |
|---|---|---|
| Fuel tank capacity (litres) | 55 | 62 |

## Engine management

Motronic ME 7.5: Fully electronic sequential injection with adaptive idle-charge control, overrun fuel cut-off, adaptive lambda control, mapped ignition with solid state high-voltage distribution, cylinder-selective adaptive knock control, air-mass measurement, integrated boost control, coordinated torque control, intake camshaft adjustment, secondary air injection.

## Suspension

Front

MacPherson struts with lower wishbones, subframe, anti-roll bar.

Rear

**FWD**: Torsion-beam rear suspension, tubular anti-roll bar
**4WD**: Longitudinal double wishbone, subframe, anti-roll bar, gas-filled shock absorbers.

## Brakes

Dual-circuit brake system with diagonal split, ABS with ESP and brake assist, brake servo, ventilated discs (front only 163/180/190 PS models). 3.2 V6 fitted with 17 inch dual-piston front brakes.

## Clutch

Manual

Hydraulically-operated, single-plate dry clutch with asbestos-free linings.

Tiptronic

Hydraulically-operated, torque converter with lock-up clutch.

DSG

Two electro hydraulically-controlled, multi-plate clutches in an oil bath.

## Steering

Rack-and-pinion steering with power assistance, steering ratio of 15.67 and turning circle of 10.6m.

## Engine

| | 163 PS | 180 PS | | 190 PS | |
|---|---|---|---|---|---|
| **Type** | 4-cylinder spark ignition engine with turbocharger, DOHC | | | | |
| | Single intercooler | Single intercooler | | Single intercooler | |

### Displacement

| | 163 PS | 180 PS | 190 PS |
|---|---|---|---|
| Capacity/bore x stroke (mm)/compression | 1781cc/8 x86.4  9.5 | 1781cc/81x86.4  9.5 | 1781cc/81x86.4  9.5 |

### Power output

| | 163 PS | 180 PS | 190 PS |
|---|---|---|---|
| (PS/RPM) | 163/5700 | 180/5500 | 190/5700 |

### Max torque

| | 163 PS | 180 PS | 190 PS |
|---|---|---|---|
| (Nm/RPM) | 225/1950-4700 | 235/1950-5000 | 240/1980-5400 |

## Drive

| | 163 PS | 180 PS FWD | 180 PS 4WD | 190 PS FWD | 190 PS 4WD |
|---|---|---|---|---|---|
| **Type** | FWD | FWD | 4WD | FWD | 4WD |
| **Gearbox** | 5-speed manual | 5-speed manual/ 6-speed tiptronic | 6-speed manual | 5-speed manual/ 6-speed tiptronic | 6-speed manual |

## Performance

| | 163 PS | 180 PS FWD | 180 PS 4WD | 190 PS FWD | 190 PS 4WD |
|---|---|---|---|---|---|
| **Max speed** (mph) | 139 | 141 | 140 | 145 | 144 |
| **0-62mph** (seconds) | 8.0 | 7.8 | 8.4 | 7.4 | 7.7 |
| **Weight** (kg) | 1280 | 1280 | 1410 | 1280 | 1410 |
| **Fuel consumption** (mpg, imperial) | | | | | |
| Urban | 25.4 | 25.4 | 21.6 | 25.4 | 21.7 |
| Extra urban | 44.8 | 44.8 | 37.2 | 44.8 | 37.6 |
| Overall | 34.8 | 34.8 | 29.7 | 34.8 | 30.0 |

| Engine | 225 PS | 240 PS Quattro Sport | 3.2 V6 |
|---|---|---|---|
| **Type** | 4-cylinder spark ignition engine with turbocharger, DOHC | | 6-cylinder spark ignition |
| | Double intercooler | Double intercooler | |
| **Displacement** | | | |
| Capacity/bore x stroke (mm)/compression | 1781cc/81x86.4 9.5 | 1781cc/81x86.4 9.5 | 3189cc/84x95.9 11.3 |
| **Power output** | | | |
| (PS/RPM) | 225/5900 | 240/5700 | 250/6300 |
| **Max torque** | | | |
| (Nm/RPM) | 280/2200-5500 | 320/2300-5000 | 320/2800-3200 |
| | | | |
| **Drive** | | | |
| **Type** | 4WD | 4WD | 4WD |
| **Gearbox** | 6speed manual | 6-speed manual | 6-speed manual/ 6-speed DSG |
| | | | |
| **Performance** | | | |
| **Max speed** (mph) | 151 | 155 | 155 |
| **0-62mph** (seconds) | 6.4 | 5.9 | 6.6 |
| **Weight** (kg) | 1465 | 1416 | 1590 |
| **Fuel consumption** (mpg, imperial) | | | |
| Urban | 23.0 | 21.2 | 20.4 |
| Extra urban | 38.7 | 39.8 | 36.2 |
| Overall | 30.7 | 30.1 | 28.2 |

# Also from Veloce Publishing ...

The **Essential** Buyer's Guide

PORSCHE
**924**
All models 1976 to 1988

Your marque expert: Steve Hodgki

978-1-845844-09-7

The **Essential** Buyer's Guide

Porsche
**911SC**
Coupé, Targa, Cabriolet & RS
Model years 1978-1983

Your marque expert: Adrian Streathe

978-1-845843-30-4

The **Essential** Buyer's Guide

Porsche
**986 BOXSTER**
Boxster, Boxster S & Boxster S 550 Spyder
Model years 1997 to 2005

Your marque expert: Adrian Streathe

978-1-845844-23-3

The **Essential** Buyer's Guide

PORSCHE
**928**

Your marque expert: David Hemmi

978-1-904788-70-6

# The Essential Buyer's Guide™ series ...

978-1-845840-22-8    978-1-845840-26-6    978-1-845840-29-7    978-1-845840-77-8    978-1-845840-99-0    978-1-904788-70-6    978-1-845841-01-0    978-1-845841-07-2

978-1-845841-19-5    978-1-845841-13-3    978-1-845841-35-5    978-1-845841-36-2    978-1-845841-38-6    978-1-845841-46-1    978-1-845841-47-8    978-1-845841-61-4

978-1-845841-63-8    978-1-845841-65-2    978-1-845841-88-1    978-1-845841-92-8    978-1-845842-00-0    978-1-845842-04-8    978-1-845842-05-5    978-1-845842-31-4

978-1-845842-70-3    978-1-845842-81-9    978-1-845842-83-3    978-1-845842-84-0    978-1-845842-87-1    978-1-84584-134-8    978-1-845843-03-8    978-1-845843-07-6

978-1-845843-09-0    978-1-845843-16-8    978-1-845843-29-8    978-1-845843-30-4    978-1-845843-34-2    978-1-845843-38-0    978-1-845843-39-7    978-1-845843-40-3

# Index

*absoluTTe* 56
Advisories 17
Air conditioning 31
Air filter 33
Alignment 19, 50
Anti-roll bar 38
Anti-lock Brake System
    (ABS) 21
Auctions 14, 42
Audi exclusive
    programme 56

Ball joints 36
Battery 20
Books and magazines
    56
Boost leaks 32, 50
Boot 31
BOSE 8, 48
Brakes 20, 35, 53
Build label 23
Bulkhead 32
Bushes 37, 50

Cambelt 39
Carpets 29
Central locking 30
Charge pipe 33
Chassis number 23, 32
Chips 19
Clubs 55
Clutch 35
Coil springs 36, 48
Concept 3
Convertible roof 26
Coolant 20
Cruise control 8, 48
CV boots 36

Dashboard 19, 23, 31
Dashpod 22
Dealer 13

Dents 19, 51
Diagnostics 21
Dimensions 57
Direct-Shift Gearbox
    (DSG) 6, 11, 54
Diverter valve (DV)
    33, 48
Doorcards 29
Doorlocks 30
Drive shafts 37
Driver Information
    System (DIS) 21, 31
Drop link 37

Electrics 39
Electronic Stability
    Program (ESP) 8, 21
Engine Control Unit
    (ECU) 18, 22
Engine number 23
Engines 40
Exhaust 19
Exterior 24

Face-lift 12
Flywheel 36
Frankfurt 3
Fuel 54
Fuel economy 58
Fuel guage 31

Gear knob 21
Glass 26

Haldex 38
Handbrake 21
Head gasket 20, 41
Headlights 19
Headlining 29
Heated seats 21
HID 27
Hoses 33, 50, 54

Induction 48
Injector seals 34
Inlet manifold 20, 41
Instrument panel 31
Insurance 6, 14

Key points 23

Lack of use 53
Laptop 18
Leather 20
LED 21, 31
Lights 26

Micro-switch 30
Modifications 13
MOT 17, 44
Motorsport 56

OBD2 16, 18
Oil 20, 33, 34, 54

Paint 24, 49, 51
Panel fit 18, 24
Pipework 35
Power steering 6, 37

QS 11
Quattro 4, 8

Registration document
    17, 19, 23, 44
Remap 48
Restoration 46, 49
Road licence 45
Running costs 7

Satellite navigation
    8, 48
Scanner 16, 18, 22
Screen washer 21
Seatbelts 28

Seats 28
Service history 45
Servicing 7, 8
Shut lines 24
Softtop 26
Software 18
Spare wheel 32
Specialists 55
Steering 19, 22, 30, 50
Strut mounts 38
Suspension 19, 48, 49
Switchgear 22

Tailgate 32
Temperature 22
Temperature gauge 31
Tensioner pulley 39
Test drive 41
Tiebars 38
Timing chain 39
Toolkit 32
Tools for inspection 16
Trackrods 36
Trim 25
TT Owners' Club 55
Turbo 20, 32, 33
Tyres 27, 54

Understeer 8
Upholstery 20

Valuation 45
Vehicle Identification
    Number (VIN) 14,
    19, 23, 32

Websites 55
Wheels 19, 27, 32
Windows 30
Wipers 26
Wiring 39
Wishbones 37